Something New with St. Thérèse

By the Author

Stations of the Cross with our Sister Saint Thérèse

Being Catholic:
What Every Catholic Should Know

Homeschooling with Gentleness

A Little Way of Homeschooling

The Paradise Project

Edited by the Author

Selected Sermons of
Thomas Aquinas McGovern, S. J.

Something New with St. Thérèse

Her Eucharistic Miracle

Suzie Andres

Little Way
B O O K S

ISBN 978-1-7347093-7-7

First printing

For all very little souls
May St. Thérèse of the Child Jesus and the Holy Face
give us a double portion of her spirit

A Prayer with St. Thérèse

My God,
If this is not Your will,
I ask You for the grace
not to be able to succeed at it.
But if this is for Your glory,
help me.

*At that time Jesus said: I give praise to You, Father,
Lord of Heaven and earth, for although You have
hidden these things from the wise and the learned
You have revealed them to the little ones.
Yes, Father, for such was Your gracious will.*

—Matthew 11:25-26

*If His Majesty should desire to raise us
to the position of one who is an intimate
and shares His secrets, we should accept gladly.*

—St. Teresa of Avila

Contents

Introduction

*And Jesus called a little child to Him, set him in their midst,
and said: Amen I say to you, unless you turn and become
like little children, you will not enter into the Kingdom
of Heaven. Whoever, therefore, humbles himself as this
little child, he is the greatest in the Kingdom of Heaven.*

—Matthew 18:2-4

On October 19, 1997, the centenary of her birth into Heaven,
Pope St. John Paul II proclaimed St. Thérèse of the Child Jesus
of the Holy Face a Doctor of the Church. In doing so he confirmed the continuous teaching of his predecessors that her Little
Way was meant for all souls, and he elevated her doctrine to the
highest possible degree.

What this Little Way is and how we can follow it, St. Thérèse
made clear in her *Story of a Soul*, in the teaching she gave to her
novices, and in the replies and statements she made in *Her Last
Conversations*, as recorded by her sisters in the last six months
before she died.

Furthermore, thanks to the apostolic letter he wrote to accompany her doctorate (*Divini Amoris Scientia* or "The Science of Divine Love"), St. John Paul II has left no doubt as to why Holy Mother Church proposes St. Thérèse's teaching to the universal Church, and exactly what she is proposing. He writes:

> The doctrine of Thérèse of Lisieux appears in providential harmony with the Church's most authentic tradition, both for its confession of the Catholic faith and for its promotion of the most genuine spiritual life, presented to all the faithful in a living, accessible language.

As to what this doctrine is and promotes, the Holy Father states:

> The core of her message is actually the mystery itself of God-Love, of the Triune God, infinitely perfect in Himself... At the summit, as the source and goal, is the merciful love of the three Divine Persons, as she expresses it, especially in her Act of Oblation to Merciful Love.

The number of books written on St. Thérèse of Lisieux in the last century, on her life, her holiness, and every conceivable aspect of her doctrine, are countless. At least I have not been able to count them, let alone read them, although I've been doing my best in this regard for the past thirty-some years.

I do not, however, apologize for writing another book on St. Thérèse. I write because, like many before me, I am compelled by her to share yet another aspect of her teaching, and in doing so assist her in her mission to make God loved as she loved Him.

I do, however, come to you at the outset of this book in order to answer an objection that I fear will, if unanswered, vitiate the purpose of what follows in these pages.

As well as being a student and disciple of St. Thérèse, I am a student and disciple of St. Thomas Aquinas. He is my confirmation Saint, the patron of my alma mater, and the Church's

Common Doctor, so named for the universality of his teaching. He is one of the first Saints I fell in love with, and he's guided my steps for at least forty years.

Frankly, though, I find his writings less accessible than Thérèse's, and one thing in particular I've never understood is why, in the *Summa* especially, St. Thomas uses the format of beginning every new question with an objection, or rather a series of objections.

Don't tell me that's what all his buddies did, so St. Thomas bowed to peer pressure. Like Mozart, he was a genius who made use of the techniques of his day, and providentially the combination of genius and technique led to the greatest theology (and music) the world has known.

Sure, the objections are helpful for seeing in what direction the question will be answered: If the objector rudely insists "Yes!" the correct answer is surely No. If the objector whines "South!" then surely the answer is North. Nonetheless, I've often skipped the objections and jumped to the body of the article to find the pith of St. Thomas' teaching, only returning to the aforesaid objections to understand their concluding replies (and sometimes seeing them simply through their replies).

Wouldn't it have made more sense for St. Thomas to present the answer first? Get to the point already, the hurried modern reader silently urges in his frustration at the Angelic Doctor's seeming lack of efficiency.

I find as I get older that Jesus has this wonderful habit of answering all my unanswered questions, satisfying one by one my silent frustrations. I don't even really have to ask, and I find that He has again provided the solution.

When I edited the *Selected Sermons of Thomas Aquinas McGovern, S.J.*, I wrote an afterword explaining the genesis of the book. Whenever I give someone a copy of this book, I tell them to read the afterword first. You'd think I made a mistake and should've put the afterword at the beginning so it could be read first without special instructions. But no, I didn't want to delay the reader's entrance into the heart of the book, the sermons themselves, nor did I want to distract the reader from the Foreword by Dr. Ronald McArthur. Finally, it doesn't help that my husband is one of those "I don't read Introductions" type of people.

I've learned my lesson. However much front matter my decision forces the reader to skip to get to the "pith" of this book, I need to put last things first, or, following the pattern set by my beloved St. Thomas, first things first. But let me explain, with more than an example of learning from my mistakes, why I need to answer an objection before I've even given you, the reader, something to which you can object.

I wrote this book some time ago. I wrote it quickly and then submitted it to an experienced Carmelite priest who is an expert on St. Thérèse. He read the book carefully and responded enthusiastically that it was excellent, true, and important. Funny, too, he thought, which made me smile as I had made him smile.

So far, so good.

The problem came when I shared the book with two close friends. At this point I wasn't trying to improve the book so much as improve their understanding of God's great love by extending the invitation that is at the heart of this book, the invitation at the heart of Thérèse's Little Way.

Their reaction? Objections.

No problem. I had a whole long chapter of objections right where it should be, around the middle of the book, just after my full proposal of Thérèse's something new and my extrapolation of her arguments for it. Since they had more objections, I simply added them to the objections chapter. Granted, a sort of middle-aged spread was taking over the central section of the book, but if that's what it took to alleviate the reader's hesitations, I wasn't about to quibble with a few extra pounds.

Until one of my dear friends admitted that she had stopped reading mid-way through. Before she even got to the objections, I think, but it didn't really matter. What mattered was that she couldn't see her way to going further in what looked like "The Little Way for Really Holy Souls."

My other friend had essentially the same problem, and here we are.

And here it is:

In this book, I bring forward a long ignored petition from St. Thérèse's Act of Oblation to Merciful Love. This Act, according to the Church, is central to her teaching, her Little Way, propelling the soul, as it does, to "the summit ... the source and goal ... the merciful love of the three Divine Persons."

Was this Act meant for only Really Holy Souls? No.

Is this Act reserved for those who have made a long preparation? No.

Is this Act one that we should *not* try at home? No.

That is, we very much should try this at home, or in church, or in a box, with a fox—anywhere, that is, that we can make it, and as soon as possible.

Here is what little Thérèse wrote in *Story of a Soul* on this question. Her sister, Mother Agnes of Jesus, to whom Thérèse had given *carte blanche* regarding the preparation, editing, and publication of her autobiography, thought this passage so important that she used it to conclude the last chapter of *Story of a Soul*. Pope Pius XI thought this text, this prayer actually, so important that he used it to conclude his homily at the canonization of our little Doctor.

Thérèse had written and prayed:

O Jesus! why can't I tell all *little* souls how unspeakable is Your condescension? I feel that if You found a soul weaker and littler than mine, which is impossible, You would be pleased to grant it still greater favors, provided it abandoned itself with total confidence to Your infinite Mercy. But why do I desire to communicate Your secrets of Love, O Jesus, for was it not You alone who taught them to me, and can You not reveal them to others? Yes, I know it and I beg You to do it. I beg You to cast Your Divine Glance upon a great number of *little* souls. I beg You to choose a legion of *little* Victims worthy of Your LOVE!

The thrice repeated emphasis on "little" comes directly from Thérèse, not me. I am merely the messenger of the messenger, and to those who will hesitate to run with Thérèse along her Little Way, I can only repeat her words to her sister Marie of the Sacred Heart, when after reading the foregoing prayer (written to Jesus, but written for her), Marie was the first of many to object that perhaps—certainly, in her estimation—this Little Way was much too great for a soul like hers. Once again (as throughout this book) the emphases are straight from Thérèse:

Dear Sister, I am not embarrassed in answering you … How can you ask me if it is possible for you to love God as I love Him?… Ah! I really feel that what pleases God in my little soul is *that He sees me loving my littleness and my poverty, the blind hope that I have in His mercy* … that is my only treasure. Why should this treasure not be yours?… Oh, dear Sister, I beg you, understand your little girl, understand that to love Jesus, to be His *victim of love*, the weaker one is, without desires or virtues, the more suited one is for the workings of this consuming and transforming Love … let us love our littleness, let us love to feel nothing, then we shall be poor in spirit, and Jesus will come to look for us, and *however far* we may be, He will transform us in flames of love … Oh! how I would like to be able to make you understand what I feel! … It is confidence and nothing but confidence that must lead us to Love ... Since we see the way, let us run together. Yes, I feel it, Jesus wills to give us the same graces, He wills to give us His Heaven *gratuitously*. (Letter 197)

Thérèse was way smarter than I am, not to mention more inspired. She had a simple procedure for convincing the little souls nearest to her that they, too, should make the Act of Oblation to Merciful Love. She didn't argue. She allowed each soul an objection or two, answered succinctly, then grabbed their hands and ran.

With her first disciple, her sister Céline, there were no objections. There was no time for objections: Thérèse literally grabbed her and ran.

For Marie of the Sacred Heart, her second inductee into the Act, she wrote the passages quoted above, but that was more than a year after she had answered Marie's initial objection that to make the Act was to invite suffering. No, said Thérèse with finality, that would be the Offering to Justice. This is the Offering to Merciful Love and it invites God's Merciful Love into the soul, not suffering.

Thérèse's third follower in this Little Way of oblation to Merciful Love was her irrepressible novice, Marie of the Trinity. When Thérèse proposed that Marie make the Act, Marie immediately consented, filled with joy. Upon an hour's reflection, however, Marie returned to Thérèse, objecting that she wasn't ready because she wasn't yet worthy and needed to do some serious preparation before taking such a big step.

Thérèse replied:

"Yes, this Act is important, more important than we can imagine, but do you know the only preparation which the good God asks of us? Well, it is that we recognize humbly our unworthiness! And since He has given you this grace, abandon yourself to Him without fear."

My bold hope is that it's never too late to begin following Thérèse in all her little ways. I've done my best to forestall the objections you'll soon make to my—to Thérèse's—to Jesus'—proposals in this book. Enough already. We'll repeat our replies as needed, but the short answer is, as St. John the Baptist said, "No one can receive anything unless it is given to him from Heaven" (John 3:27). Jesus wants to give you His infinite Love; following Thérèse, I must trust Him to make it happen.

One of those two objecting friends, the one whose patroness is St. Mary Magdalene, put it best: "If Jesus was in the room, I'd throw myself at His feet in a heartbeat. But if you asked me to come meet Him next Tuesday, I'd have time to fear and I wouldn't know how to approach Him."

Jesus wants you not at His feet, but leaning upon His Sacred Heart.

He is knocking.

Turn the page, open the door, and let Him in.

Part I

Something New in St. Thérèse

Chapter 1

Thérèse's Outrageous Idea

This is the property of love: To seek out all the good things of the Beloved.

—St. John of the Cross, *Living Flame of Love*

My discovery of something new in St. Thérèse began when I went to a talk by Fr. Michael Gaitley, author of *33 Days to Morning Glory*, the book on Marian consecration that's sold over two million copies. The day I heard him, Fr. Gaitley was speaking about another book, one he had just published on St. Thérèse and Divine Mercy. At his talk, not only did he say somewhere near 700 true things about St. Thérèse, he also had books available—he smilingly explained that due to a mistake they were *free* books—and we were all invited to take one for ourselves, and one for a friend ...

My enthusiasm for St. Thérèse having been re-ignited, I got two copies and went home. The new book, *33 Days to Divine Mercy*, prepared the reader for a consecration to Merciful Love. This consecration followed the inspiration of Thérèse's "Act of

Oblation to Merciful Love," which appeared in full toward the back of the book.

Fr. Gaitley suggested we spend 33 days preparing to offer ourselves to Merciful Love in the spirit of St. Thérèse, but since I had made this offering repeatedly over the years, I felt free to skip the 33 days and instead race through his book in a single night. Not that I could absorb everything, but I felt I didn't have time to lose. And so in the wee hours of the morning, as I reached the last pages, I found myself a few steps further along the Little Way, and re-reading Thérèse's Act of Oblation to Merciful Love. And I knew that I needed to think harder about this beautiful prayer.

I began by praying it slowly and trying to mean every word. Over the next weeks I read in other books about the small changes and additions Thérèse had made to the prayer after she first composed it. Finally, I used a French dictionary to help me better understand each word of the Act in Thérèse's original French version.

At some point in my immersion into this prayer—about three weeks in—I realized what Thérèse was really saying. Again, not that I absorbed it all or actually succeeded in understanding and meaning every word I prayed, but I realized at least one of the things she was saying, and it was what I have come to think of as An Outrageous Idea.

Thérèse had plenty of impressive ideas, and given that she's a Doctor of the Church, that's not surprising. (On the other hand, given that she died at twenty-four, it's pretty awesome she's in the same class as St. Augustine, St. Thomas Aquinas, St. Francis de Sales, and the others.) But even for Thérèse, this idea is wonderful. Better yet, spectacular. Or actually, to be specific, outrageous. I've never come across an official classification of Thérèse's ideas, but I think, for our purposes, we can rank them in precisely this way:

First, we have Thérèse's wonderful ideas.

Next are her spectacular ideas.

And finally, we come to her outrageous ideas, which I also think of as the miraculous ones.

Her wonderful ideas (which would, for the rest of us, if we came up with just one, be the idea of a lifetime, but for a Doctor of the Church these come frequently) include the realizations that God had shown her graces as marvelous as those He lavished on repentant sinners, for His love prevented her from sinning at the outset; and that the Blessed in Heaven feel for us tremendous compassion since they know from experience what we are suffering.

Her spectacular ideas (impressive even for a Doctor of the Church) include her deep conviction that Divine Love has more need of victims than does Divine Justice, and also her solution to the dilemma of her "infinite" desires, which in some cases conflicted with each other and in others were impossible (for instance, her desire to suffer every kind of martyrdom for love of Jesus). Her inspired conclusion—that she will be love in the heart of the Church, for "love comprises all vocations"—is nothing short of spectacular.

Finally, we come to her outrageous ideas. These are in a class by themselves. When commentators notice her outrageous ideas, these are the ones that provoke footnotes of the qualifying sort, the implication being that she couldn't possibly have meant what she said. Even her enthusiasts find these ideas hard to take. For her part, she happily admits that she loves to the point of folly, and she does not apologize for the outrageous ideas to which her love leads her.

But also in this category there are, as well as ideas that provoke stern footnotes, ideas that go so far over our heads that we barely catch a glimpse of them. In the case of the outrageous idea I'm about to present, I've only been able to find a few pages of commentary, and even these comments are tucked into works with larger agendas.

For myself, after years of acquaintance with Thérèse's writings and a particular familiarity with the prayer containing this new idea, I've only recently begun to see what she, in very clear language, is getting at. And as the Holy Spirit unveils for me her meaning, I keep asking myself if this could even be possible.

I find her outrageous ideas also miraculous because it took a miracle for St. Thérèse to think of them, it takes a miracle for us to believe her, and it will take even more miracles for us to live these ideas as she, so miraculously, did.

She would be the first, after her Divine Master, to tell us that miracles are not a problem. If we're going to venture along the Little Way, to believe and then believe a little more in Love, we have not only to put up with miracles, but to start expecting them. Presumption is not something we have time to worry about, given all God has in store for us. As Thérèse puts it: "We can never have too much confidence in the good God; He is so mighty and so merciful. We obtain from Him as much as we hope for" (*Letters of St. Thérèse of Lisieux*, Vol. II, p. 1000).

Outrageous as this sounds—that we will obtain from God as much as we hope for—Thérèse has good reason to think so. She is simply taking her Teacher at His word. The whole collection of her ideas—wonderful, spectacular, outrageous and miraculous—comes from the same source: the Holy Spirit inspiring her to understand and take literally what Jesus told us.

And He, who can neither deceive nor be deceived, told us plainly:

"Ask and you shall receive" (Matthew 7:7) and "Be not afraid, little flock, for it has pleased your Father to give you the kingdom" (Luke 12:32). And then the night before He died, in a series of heartfelt expressions each more tender and urgent than the last, He promised: "Whatever you ask in My name, that I will do ... If you ask Me anything in my name, I will do it ... If you abide in Me and My words abide in you, ask whatever you will and it shall be done to you. In this is My Father glorified, that you bear very much fruit ... You have not chosen me, but I have chosen you and have appointed you that you should go and bear fruit, and that your fruit should remain, that whatever you ask the Father in My name He may give you ... Amen, amen I say to you, if you ask the Father anything in My name, He will give it to you. Hitherto you have not asked anything in My name. Ask, and you shall receive, that your joy may be full... In that day you shall ask in My name, and I don't say that I will ask the Father for you, for the Father Himself loves you because you have loved Me and have believed that I came forth from God" (John 14:13, 14; 15:7-8, 16; 16:23-24, 26-27).

We are all too ready to put qualifications on Jesus' statements. All of us, that is, except the Saints. And among the Saints, Thérèse is the most daring, the most confident, the one who most cherished His saying that to enter His kingdom we must be as little children. So as a child, she says to Him the words that come so naturally to a child: "You promised."

Here are the words she uses in her "Act of Oblation to the Merciful Love of the Good God" to address first the Father, and then the Son, when she boldly asks—enough stalling—for the "something new" I have found, the something new she alone would dare dream of and confidently request:

> My Beloved Spouse told us in the days of His mortal life: "Whatsoever you ask the Father in My Name He will give it to you!" I am certain, then, that You will grant my desires. I know, O my God! that the more You want to give, the more You make us desire. I feel in my heart immense desires and it is with confidence I ask You to come take possession of my soul. Ah! I cannot receive Holy Communion as often as I desire, but Lord, are You

not all-powerful? Remain in me as in a tabernacle and never separate Yourself from Your little victim.

She reminds Him of His promise to give her whatever she asks, and she does not stand on ceremony. Like the child that she is, by nature and grace, she names exactly what she wants, but only after patiently explaining to her loving Father that He started this game. He said she could have whatever she wanted, and she wants Jesus to remain in her, "as in a tabernacle." This should not be a problem for God. Is He not all-powerful?

This is the request, the demand, the outrageous idea that has captured my heart. I keep returning to it, sure I'm missing something, wondering how Thérèse can be asking what she seems to be asking. Her idea seems nothing short of outrageous and, to be blunt, I keep thinking she's gone too far. Finally, she must have come up with something God will have to refuse. And yet, she argues so persuasively. Is He not all-powerful?

When one is up against the seemingly impossible, it helps to remember the words of the Angel Gabriel: "Nothing shall be impossible with God" (Luke 1:37).

But first, let's be sure Thérèse meant what she said. Granted the Doctors of the Church tend to speak in earnest, yet given the outrageousness of her petition and the nearly universal lack of awe (certainly the lack of commentary) it has inspired, let's be sure we understand what Thérèse is requesting.

Fortunately for us, when the Church gathered witnesses to testify during the process of her canonization, Thérèse's sister and superior, Mother Agnes, was asked point blank whether Thérèse meant these words literally. Here is the relevant passage from Mother Agnes' testimony:

Mother Agnes: It was on 9 June 1895, the Feast of the Holy Trinity, that she officially made this offering of herself. I find two quite extraordinary requests in the act of offering: 1. The favor of retaining the Real Presence of Our Lord within her between one Communion and the next: "Stay in Me as You are in the tabernacle." 2. The favor of seeing the Holy Wounds of the Passion shining on her glorified body when she went to Heaven.

The judge asked if these words about "Real Presence between one Communion and the next" and "the Wounds on her glorified body" were meant in some metaphorical sense or were meant to be taken literally.

Mother Agnes: She often enlarged on these ideas when speaking to me, and I am certain she meant them literally. Her loving confidence in Our Lord made her extraordinarily daring in the things she asked Him for. When she thought of His all-powerful love, she had no doubts about anything. (*St. Thérèse of Lisieux by those who knew her, testimonies from the process of beatification*, edited and translated by Christopher O. Mahony, O.C.D.)

From Mother Agnes' testimony, we can be sure, then, that Thérèse meant what she said. When she prayed, "Remain in me as in a tabernacle," she was asking Jesus to stay in her in His Real Presence. That is, she did not want His precious Body and Blood to remain in her only fifteen minutes or so after Communion, until the host dissolved entirely. Love is not satisfied with the departure of the Beloved, and He had told her she could have whatever she asked. She asked, then, that He miraculously conserve the Sacred Species within her, so that He would remain in her as the consecrated Host—which is Him—remains in the tabernacle.

In a book published about the time of Thérèse's canonization, we find further confirmation that she meant her petition literally. The French Dominican theologian Henry Petitot, in *St.*

Teresa of Lisieux, A Spiritual Renascence, offers this explanation by Mother Agnes:

> I am certain that in this prayer she was thinking of a miraculous permanence of the sacred species, and not merely of the permanence of the divine influence, which is produced without any miracle in the souls of the faithful. Besides, in her Act of Oblation, she appeals on this point to the omnipotence of Jesus Christ.

We are, unfortunately, all too accustomed to miracles in the lives of the Saints.

Don't get me wrong: I'm glad we believe and have these signs to shore up our faith, but as true believers we can become so blasé about the wondrous that we no longer wonder at it. Part of Thérèse's charm is her ability to surprise us by the audacity of her holy daring. She has been behind innumerable miracles, the intercessor with a bucket of roses in one hand and Jesus' hand in her other. She, for one, never gets tired of the miraculous.

In order for a person to be canonized by the Church, documentable miracles (usually miraculous physical healings) have to occur at the intercession of the Blessed *after* the beatification ceremony. This ensures that God has desired the universal glorification of the Saint, that is, that the Saint be proposed as an example and Heavenly intercessor for the whole world.

In Thérèse's case, the Church shortened the time then required between her death and the opening of her cause, as it recently did for Mother Teresa and for the same reason: so that the universal veneration of the people would not precede the careful judgment of the Church. After Thérèse entered eternal life, God worked so many miracles at her request that in a few years the Carmel of Lisieux had filled several volumes with miraculous reports. None of these, however, could be used after her beatification. Her canonization required two fresh miracles.

(In more recent years, the process has been streamlined so that only one miracle is required after beatification, not two; also the waiting time before a process can be opened is now five years after death, rather than the twenty-five years it used to be.)

On the day of her beatification, witnesses recorded thirty miraculous healings through the intercession of Blessed Thérèse and reported them to the Lisieux Carmel. Thérèse was in a hurry to make God loved, and He was happy, as always, to oblige her.

And yet, which is more wonderful: Miraculous physical healings or the miracles of grace that convert and draw souls into the intimate life of the Blessed Trinity?

With my discovery of a new miracle in Thérèse, I came across the invitation she always extends: that we too should love God as she does. On July 17, 1895, she had told her sisters this would be her mission: "I feel that I'm about to enter into my rest. But I feel especially that my mission is about to begin, my mission of making God loved as I love Him, of giving my little way to souls" (*Last Conversations*, 102).

Thérèse is an apostle as well as a contemplative, and she had no desire to say her prayers alone. After her initial spontaneous offering of herself to Merciful Love, she immediately grabbed her sister Céline (known in the monastery as Sister Geneviéve) and dragged her to their older sister Pauline (Mother Agnes). Her face shining, Thérèse asked permission for herself and Céline to make an official offering of themselves to Merciful Love. When Mother Agnes consented, Thérèse set to work formally writing out her offering. Two days later, on June 11, 1895, she and Céline knelt before the Virgin of the Smile and made the offering together.

Not long after, Thérèse approached her sister and godmother, Marie of the Sacred Heart, and asked her, too, to make the Offering. Marie objected that she had no desire to ask God for more suffering, which inspired Thérèse to explain that this was an offering to Love, not Justice, and Marie had nothing to fear. Marie consented.

The following November, Thérèse recruited her novice, Marie of the Trinity.

In *Story of a Soul*, at the end of Chapter IX we can read the desires of Thérèse's heart, which burned to set the world on fire with love for Jesus. She writes:

> O Jesus! why can't I tell all little souls how unspeakable is Your condescension? I feel that if You found a soul weaker and littler than mine, which is impossible, You would be pleased to grant it still greater favors, provided it abandoned itself with total confidence to Your Infinite Mercy. But why do I desire to communicate Your secrets of Love, O Jesus, for was it not You alone who taught them to me, and can You not reveal them to others? Yes, I know it, and I beg You to do it. I beg You to cast Your Divine Glance upon a great number of little souls. I beg You to choose a legion of little Victims worthy of Your LOVE! (p. 200)

In other words, Thérèse not only has an outrageous new idea, but she wants us to live it with her, she wants Jesus to make it happen not only in her life, but in ours.

St. Thérèse has, actually, three requests related to her "something new."

First, she wants Jesus to remain in her as in a tabernacle.

Second, she wants us to make this prayer with her (for she wants us to make the Act of Oblation, and this petition is contained within it).

Third, she wants Jesus Himself to teach and effect in us the secrets of His Love, including this one.

Is this too much? I have often wondered, and in my recent awe and perplexity, I decided Thérèse needed reinforcements. And so, in order to confirm the possibility of her latest outrageous idea, I decided to gather all the evidence I could find. Although in Thérèse's life, "without showing Himself, without making His voice heard, Jesus teaches me in secret," (*Story of a Soul*, p. 187), He has not always been so subtle. Were there other Saints who lived this Eucharistic miracle? By God's grace, yes, and in His tender compassion, I found them.

Chapter 2

God's Idea First

Behold, I am doing something new.
Now it springs forth, do you not perceive it?

—Isaiah 43:19

Having discovered this outrageous new idea in St. Thérèse, I wanted to find confirmation in the lives of other Saints. It seemed a good place to look, for God speaks through His Saints in many ways. Not least of which is in the beautiful miracles of grace He works in their souls, where He shows us what it delights Him to do in those completely surrendered to Him.

St. Thérèse has a wonderful expression, "For simple souls, there are no complicated ways." For myself, as too often happens with her sayings, the reverse is more true. Thus in typical complicated-soul fashion, I did not take the easy route to finding the confirmation for which I looked.

In Fr. Gaitley's book, which put me back in touch with St. Thérèse and her Act of Oblation, the endnotes are marvelous. I knew this because the night I read the book, I also read the endnotes. Next to endnote 121, I put a heart in the margin.

One problem with reading a book as fast as I like to, is that retention can be a little iffy. And so, as the weeks passed after that fateful glorious night of reading, I was sure I needed to start from scratch in finding confirmation of this miracle in the lives of the Saints.

My husband and sons and I like to go on "family dates" to Barnes and Noble. Browsing through the religion section one evening about two months after I'd begun hoping and looking, I found Vinny Flynn's *7 Secrets of the Eucharist*. Flipping through it, I came upon the first confirmation I needed—he had an excerpt from St. Faustina's *Diary*, in which she wrote:

> I have come to know that Holy Communion remains in me until the next Holy Communion. A vivid and clearly felt presence of God continues in my soul ... My heart is a living tabernacle in which the living Host is reserved. (*Diary*, 1302)

I was thrilled. I had known it must be: someone other than Thérèse must have experienced this miracle of the conservation of the Sacred Species, and here was evidence! I wasn't surprised that it was St. Faustina. Later I found another passage in her *Diary* confirming this miracle of grace: "After Holy Communion, I saw Jesus in the same way in my heart and felt Him physically in my heart throughout the day" (434).

Having found the first confirmation, the very direct words of Our Lord to Faustina, I was eager for others. I hoped to catch a glimmer of the miracle in St. Padre Pio. Knowing his intense intimacy with Jesus, I was sure God had given Pio this gift too, though leafing through my biographies and books of excerpts from his letters, I found nothing.

I have a little book called *Padre Pio's Mass* by Fr. Tarcisio of Cervinara. I don't how I acquired the book—it comes from Our Lady of Grace Friary, San Giovanni Rotondo, where Padre Pio lived and where I've never been. I had previously read snippets of the book, and about this time I wanted to re-read a lovely passage about Holy Communion. Father Tarcisio writes that Padre Pio was asked, "What is Holy Communion?" and he responded "It is all an internal and external mercy. An embrace. Ask Jesus to make Himself felt sensibly."

"Where does Jesus kiss you?"

"All over."

"When Jesus comes does He visit only the soul?"

"The whole being."

"What does Jesus do at Communion?"

"He finds delight in His creature."

"Is Communion an incorporation?"

"It is a fusion. Like two candles that melt together and are no longer distinguishable."

This much of the interchange I had read before, and I picked the book up again simply to re-read it to remind myself of Padre Pio's words, especially his answer to "What does Jesus do at Communion?"—"He finds delight in His creature."

But now, holding the book, I turned the page and read on. It was two weeks after my discovery in St. Faustina. Here is what I found in Padre Pio:

"You have made me understand that the Sacred Species are not consumed in you; that the Blood of Jesus flows in your veins! Therefore you are a living monstrance?"

"You have said it!"

It was the only mention I had seen of this miracle in Padre Pio, but it was explicit and direct. It also echoed a beautiful stanza in St. Thérèse's poem, "My Desires Near Jesus Hidden in His Prison of Love," in which she sings:

> Holy Paten, I envy you.
> Upon you, Jesus comes to rest.

> Oh! may His infinite grandeur
> Deign to humble Itself even to me ...
> Fulfilling my hope, Jesus
> Does not wait until the evening of my life.
> He comes within me, by His presence
> I am a living Monstrance!...

My hunch was right. Jesus, who loved Pio so much, could not deny him, too, this grace. Later I discovered further confirmation in St. Pio's prayer, "O Mother Most Sweet," in which he asks Mary, "Purify my body so that I may be His living tabernacle!" And now, though perhaps another researcher might have been satisfied, I only felt inspired to look for more instances. Not in Pio; I had what I needed there, but in other Saints as well.

Four months passed. On the 26th of August, 2016, Carmelite feast of the Transverberation of St. Teresa of Avila's heart, I entered St. Sebastian's Church in Santa Paula for my 11:00 a.m. Friday holy hour. I had brought a booklet called "Eucharistic Adoration for the Sanctification of Priests and Spiritual Maternity," published by the Vatican's Congregation for the Clergy, because I remembered a beautiful colloquy in the back of the booklet, designed to help the adorer pray in a holy hour. Turning to the colloquy, I read this introductory paragraph by St. Anthony Mary Claret (which paragraph actually had little to do with the "conversation with Jesus" that he had written and which followed):

> On 26 August 1861, finding myself at prayer in the Church of the Holy Rosary, at La Granja, at seven o'clock in the evening, the Lord granted me the grace of conserving the Sacramental Species within my heart. I now bear within me day and night the adorable Eucharist. I must therefore be always recollected and cultivate the interior life.

I was in awe. I thanked Jesus and wondered … and it wasn't until that night, when I told my husband of the experience and read aloud to him St. Anthony Mary Claret's words, that I realized the Holy Spirit had given me this passage on the anniversary of the day St. Anthony received this grace.

A few days later I was in the stacks of St. Bernardine Library at Thomas Aquinas College to check out a book on St. Thérèse. I stood amidst shelves and shelves of books on the lives and writings of the Saints. "Won't one of you help me?" I pleaded quietly. "I know there are more of you here, but who are you?"

I saw the appealing cream-colored spine of an old soft cover book; it was the title, really, that attracted me: *Canticle of Love.* I pulled the book off the shelf and read its cover. The subtitle was "Autobiography of Marie Sainte-Cecile de Rome, R.J.M. (Dina Belanger), 1897-1929." The book came from the Convent of Jesus and Mary, Sillery, Quebec, Canada. The name Dina Belanger rang a faint bell, but I put the book back on the shelf, saying to myself as I'd said often enough, "If you pull out every book, you'll never get anywhere!" (Though often enough I'd had to return for the book I originally passed by.)

More promising on this particular day were several books one shelf over from *Canticle of Love,* books on the life and miracles of St. Anthony Mary Claret. One was his autobiography. Why not see if I could find the passage on his Eucharistic miracle? I knew the date—August 26, 1861—and part of the book was written like a diary. Sure enough, I found the entry easily. This translation read:

> When I was praying in the Church of the Rosary in La Granja, on the 26th of August at 7 o'clock in the evening, Our Lord granted me the great grace of retaining the sacramental species. Day and night I have the Most Holy Sacrament in my breast. For this reason, I must always be

recollected and devoted to Him who abides so intimately within me. (p. 180)

I stood in the stacks, again lost in wonder. Jesus wanted his Saints to experience His sacramental Presence constantly; the message was making it, slowly, through my thick skull. But then I shook my head. This seemed crazy. How could I be sure?

I re-read the passage and decided to keep reading. On the next page, I found the validation I longed for. St. Anthony had written:

On the 16th of May [1862] at 4:15, while I was in prayer, the same thing occurred of which I made mention before in this chapter, namely, the conservation of the Blessed Sacrament in my breast. Yesterday, and today also, I was thinking of erasing from this autobiography what I had written concerning this, but the Blessed Virgin told me not to do so. Afterwards at Mass, Jesus Christ told me that He had granted me the grace of His always remaining sacramentally within me. (p. 181)

St. Anthony, the Blessed Mother, and Our Lord had conspired to reassure me. I checked out the books on this wonderful Saint, brought them home, and they sat on my desk.

Life rushed along, and the canonization of Mother Teresa was fast approaching. I planned to celebrate it as I celebrate many canonizations: by finding something to read about her on the day and thus rejoicing at home while the universal Church celebrated in Rome and around the world.

As I prepared to return to the library for books on Mother Teresa, I noticed in my breviary a little note I'd written the previous year: "September 4: Blessed Dina Belanger." That was why her name had rung a bell—she was a Canadian Blessed I'd discovered and then (such is the poverty of my memory) fairly soon forgotten. Mother Teresa would be canonized on Blessed Dina's day, so I decided to check out Dina's book too, in preparation for "their" feast.

It was the work of a pleasant afternoon, and then *Canticle of Love* rested on a table with the Mother Teresa books. September 4th arrived, and I still hadn't started reading. I awoke early in the morning with a sudden inspiration about where I could watch the canonization that night, or really the next morning, at 1 a.m. our time, when it would be 9 a.m. in Rome. I said a novena prayer to St. Thérèse and started laughing.

I'd already missed it! This was September 4th, the day of the canonization, which meant it had happened hours before! So much for "being there" even virtually. God had other plans ...

That night after dinner I realized I still hadn't opened any of the books I'd checked out. I knew I had the next day to keep celebrating Mother Teresa, for September 5th would be her first feast day as "St. Mother Teresa" here below, but it struck me that Blessed Dina was waiting, and if I didn't look at her book now, I'd never get to it. I picked up *Canticle of Love* and whispered a prayer: "You know I don't have much time, and this is a fat book. If it's in here, show me."

I flipped open to a random page and saw that some of the paragraphs were italicized. I read something about a chalice, and realized that the italicized words were those spoken by Our Lord to Dina—I hadn't expected this.

"Okay, then, you know I don't have much time," I repeated, and flipped to another page. There I read:

> "*The grace of my chalice,* said He, *is My real presence that I give you, as in the Sacred Host. I already told you this but I allowed you not to understand fully. You possess Me constantly and really, as during the instants that follow your Sacramental Communion. My power and goodness are infinite. It is just as easy for Me to give Myself to you*

really by an intimate interior grace, invisible to all, as it is
for Me to conceal Myself in the consecrated Host or in the
chalice on the altar, under the appearance of wine. My little
spouse, I love you. Because I love you, I wish to lavish My
graces upon you with prodigal generosity. And always for
the same purpose: the glory of My Father, the consolation
of My Heart, and the salvation and sanctification of souls."
(*Canticle of Love*, entry for April 5, 1928, p. 262)

I cried.

My husband was sitting a few feet away, and I told him of
my book and my prayer, and then read aloud to him what I had
just read to myself. It was nice to have one of these miracles of
discovery happen with a witness.

It was Blessed Dina's feast, and she was as accommodating
as St. Anthony Mary Claret had been on the anniversary of his
special day. I have long known the friendship of the Saints for
us, but it was an added miracle to have their kindness confirmed
along with this outrageous miracle of the Eucharist.

As an added bonus, several months later I discovered this
same miracle in the lives of two holy mystics, Sister Jeanne Benigne Gojos and Sister Gertrude Mary, who had been mentioned
by St. Anthony Mary Claret's biographers when they were looking for similar confirmations in the lives of the saints.

Later still, a friend found this telling line in *The Autobiog-*
raphy of St. Margaret Mary: "My Sovereign Lord continued to
favour me with His real and sensible Presence, which grace, as
I said above, He promised would not be withdrawn from me."

The only conclusions I can make are the following:

First, that Jesus' love truly knows no bounds and He continually seeks a more perfect union with us.

Second, that St. Thérèse was neither the first nor the last to
experience this miracle of the conservation of the Holy Eucharist
in the soul between Communions.

But third, there are two interesting differences between St. Thérèse and Sts. Faustina, Anthony Mary Claret, Margaret Mary, and Blessed Dina. Little Thérèse is the only one of this group who does not offer us verification (through private revelation) of this miracle in her soul: we have not the words of Our Lord to her, but rather the words of her to Our Lord. And this is, in fact, the adorable second difference between Thérèse and the others: As far as I can tell, Thérèse alone, bold child of her holy Mother St. Teresa (whom the poet Crashaw rightly called "undaunted daughter of desires"), dared to ask for this miracle for herself. And she alone, as far as I have seen, urges us to make this invitation our own.

If it seems outrageous that she asks for herself, what can we say about her encouragement that we, too, ask for this grace-beyond-imagining? In her defense, I will conclude this chapter by saying that it was God's idea first, and, as usual, little Thérèse is merely dreaming big and trusting her all-powerful and all-loving Father to fulfill His promises. Not that He promised this miracle specifically, nor that she knew He had the idea first. She simply had confidence, following the doctrine of St. John of the Cross, that her desires came from God, and He gave them in order to fulfill them.

As to the matter of her inviting us to share her desires and her absolute confidence in their fulfillment in us, we will have more to say in the upcoming chapters.

Incidentally, endnote 121 of Fr. Gaitley's *33 Days to Merciful Love* informs the inquiring reader: "Like the Saint of the Little Way, St. Faustina also received the grace of having Holy Communion remain within her," and Fr. Gaitley goes on to quote the passage (from September 29, 1937) in her *Diary* which I later found quoted by Vinny Flynn. I long ago learned not to deprecate the weakness of my memory. It gives me so much to be grateful for, again and again.

Part II

Something New for Us?

Chapter 3

Céline's Conviction and the Biggest Objection

Then she wrote about the Act of Oblation in her
autobiography, and invited all little souls to share her riches.

—Céline (*Memoir of My Sister, St. Thérèse*)

In the first part of this book, we saw that while Thérèse came up with a more than wonderful, more than spectacular, truly outrageous idea and went with it, God Himself was (as usual) the initiator. Given St. Anthony Mary Claret's experience of Jesus remaining within him in the Eucharist between Communions—which Jesus effected and revealed to him thirty-five years before Thérèse prayed for this grace—we can say that this was God's idea first.

In *Story of a Soul*, St. Thérèse prays boldly for a double portion of the spirit of the Saints. Since at least one Saint had experienced the conservation of the Blessed Sacrament within himself, this was among the graces Thérèse asked for, albeit in a universal, all-encompassing request. And, true to form, while in her littleness and ordinary way she didn't receive an audible or visual message from Jesus regarding His fulfillment of her prayer that He remain within her as in a tabernacle, she believed with full confidence that He answered her petition.

The question before us now is whether we too ought to follow her along this particular path. It's all well and good, charming, wholesome, safe and, by now, familiar to follow in her Little Way. But this particular stretch of her path is likely more than we bargained for.

It may help to review the history of St. Thérèse's way of trust.

Céline, the sister whom Thérèse said was like a salad well-seasoned with vinegar and spices, practically strong armed the Church authorities when it came to the question of the Little Way. Thérèse had died in 1897. A few years later her process began. The first phase was to gather testimonies from the living witnesses of her life. The nuns of her monastery carefully prepared statements. These testimonies would be given under oath, meaning that deviation from the truth was perjury, and the witness liable to excommunication.

When Céline gave her testimony, she was asked, "Why do you desire the Beatification of Sister Thérèse of the Child Jesus?" She responded that the only reason she desired Thérèse's Beatification was in order to promulgate her Little Way. The Promoter of the Faith warned her to drop the subject, saying, "Once you begin to speak of a special *Way*, the Cause is infallibly doomed; innumerable cases on record bear abundant witness to that" (*Memoir of My Sister, St. Thérèse*, p. 39).

The intrepid Céline remained unabashed, replying, "That is indeed too bad, but a fear of hindering the Beatification of Sister Thérèse could never deter me from stressing the only important point that interests me—that her *Little Way* might be raised with her, so to speak, to the honors of the altar." Céline would not be silenced because there was no point in promoting the cause unless it would further Thérèse's mission.

Far from sinking the cause, Thérèse's Little Way (and Céline's insistence upon it) became not only compelling evidence for Thérèse's sanctity, but a mandate the Church offered for the sanctity of all her children. Céline rejoiced when in 1921 Pope Benedict XV, proclaiming Thérèse's heroic virtue, preached on her way of spiritual childhood and recommended it in the highest possible terms as a sure path to holiness for all the faithful.

The original "innovation" of Thérèse's Little Way can seem, more than 120 years after she discovered it and a century after the Church first recommended it, less than new. It has a homey, familiar air to it, like her Shower of Roses. But like a rose received from Thérèse at the end of a novena (or a roomful of roses, as a skeptic I knew once found waiting for her), the Little Way can still take us unawares—we think we know it, or have the general idea, but that's different from living it day to day with all its implications.

Jesus said, long before St. Thérèse did, "You must become as little children." We nod and smile, "Yes. Definitely. Like little children. Sounds like a plan." But what does He mean? This was Thérèse's specialty, and she's an excellent guide to the spiritual childhood Jesus recommended in no uncertain terms.

She is now a Doctor of the Church. This is a huge deal. We take it for granted that her holy parents in Carmel, St. John of the Cross and St. Teresa of Avila, are Doctors of the Church, but it took over 300 years for John's doctorate to be proclaimed, and almost 400 years for Teresa's. With little Thérèse, everything happens quickly. She was in a hurry and still is: no time to lose in making Love loved. After all, Our Lord Himself said: "See, I come quickly; I have My reward in hand" (Rev 21:12).

For those who knew her, who were converted through her writings, who had been recipients not only of her roses but of her doctrine, the 100 years it took seemed very long to wait for her doctorate. In the life of the Church, though, it was a flash, and now here she stands, the youngest of the Doctors, not twenty-five years old, but savvy with the wisdom of the ages.

Her doctorate makes a difference because Thérèse says some wild things, and there's no point spending a lifetime trying to understand and live her prescriptions unless we are sure she is right.

We are sure.

So, then, back to her little way of spiritual childhood: Here Thérèse is recommending absolute confidence in God our Father. Confidence in His goodness and love for us, but that means confidence that He will give us what we ask. And now she is encouraging us to ask Him for Jesus to remain within us as in a tabernacle.

The Church tells us to trust Thérèse, to follow her, to imitate her. Granted, with other Saints we must be careful not to imitate everything. While the Church recommends these heroes of the Faith for our edification, there is often a "don't try this at home" warning that doesn't even need to be stated aloud. St. Simon Stylites sat atop a pillar for twenty years. St. Francis of Assisi confronted a ferocious wolf; St. Anthony of Padua commanded the fish to rise to the surface of the water to hear his sermon; St. Rose of Lima invited the mosquitoes to separate into two "choirs" and buzz along with her recitation of the Divine Office. Several of the Saints lived for years on only the nourishment of the Blessed Sacrament. We would be entertaining delusions of grandeur to think we were called to imitate these Saints in the particulars.

So what about St. Thérèse and this new idea of hers? It looks like it falls into the class of "insanely amazing wonders God performs in the lives of the greatest Saints but don't get presumptuous, Johnny." What makes us think this outrageous miracle is for us—I mean for us to live?

For starters, St. Thérèse wanted to be imitable in everything. Toward the end of her life, when her mission was becoming clearer to her, when she knew that God would have her teaching this Little Way not only to her novices and spiritual brothers, but to the whole world, she spoke frequently about the necessity that everything about her way be truly little, and thus imitable. She said to a friend, "In my Little Way all things are common and ordinary. It is necessary that all that I do, little souls should be able to do also" (*Complete Spiritual Doctrine of St. Thérèse of Lisieux*, p. 121).

This did not mean she limited her desires. And if you think about it, this makes sense, because desires are the one thing that, even as little ones, we can have hugely.

I have two sons. (I had desired a large family, and God gave it to me: my boys were born twelve years apart, and this makes for a large family in duration, if not in number. Also, like every mother worth her salt, I'm convinced my boys are worth twenty average children, so I have no complaints.) From infancy, my younger son had quite strong desires. For instance, when it was time to sleep, he would resist with all his little might because the world was so interesting to him. There was so much (you could tell) he already wanted to do (even though he couldn't yet do much at all), and sleep seemed to him like death. As he got older, say into toddlerhood, he was quite passionate about many things. He was packed full of desires. And it helped me to realize that while he was having trouble being three, he would soon come into his own: he would be a fabulous thirty-year-old, if we could just get through the intervening years.

Thérèse was like this too. While she believed in remaining little, her littleness was never a restraint on her desires. She believed in desires being immense, at the very least. Not because we are capable of attaining great things. No, her message is that of ourselves we are much smaller than we can ever imagine. But God is very, very big, and so not only does our littleness attract—and provide the perfect stage for—His infinite mercy and power, but also our desires, since we are asking Him to fulfill them, must be nearly infinite (she would leave out the "nearly") in order to match what He can and wants to give us.

We can read in the lives of the mystics, and more plainly in the writings of the Mystical Doctor, St. John of the Cross, that God wants for us nothing less than our divinization. I'm not going to address that here, for two reasons. First, it would get us off track—we're supposed to be talking about whether we can want, with Thérèse, this one specific miracle from God (probably not unrelated to divinization). Second, I would have to do a lot more research, studying, and learning to be able to know what in the world I'm talking about. So, in the interest of time (I'm on Thérèse's side and therefore in a hurry too), let's just say that God has huge plans for us. There is no need to worry that our desires will outrun His.

All of this makes clear to me why the Carmelite priest to whom I first mentioned Thérèse's "something new" told me to go deeper with this Saint. She's so terrific that there's plenty to be gained by any degree of acquaintance with her. To know her a little is already to have learned a lot—even a smile from a saint is a great gift, full of God's love. So I'm right there alongside those who say the occasional novena to her (I think of it as a proper novena if I forget a day or two, thus making it a "little" novena) and I'm equally grateful, my trust in God increased, when I get a rose at the end of the day. But I'm suggesting there's something more to which she invites us: I think she's ready for us to go deeper with her—I know we are little, we can't even say all nine days of a novena, at least not consecutively, but I'm still convinced she wants us to acknowledge our littleness not in order to shy away from Love's advances, but as a reason to believe all the more. Because this is really about how much God loves us, not about how little we love Him.

Which brings us back to the question we must now begin to answer.

Granted the Church proposes St. Thérèse as a guide for us. Is Thérèse, our guide, now proposing that we, too, ask God to remain in us as in a tabernacle?

Yes, she is, and there is so much proof that hopefully it will overcome our monstrous doubts. Or perhaps I should say mountainous doubts, for it occurs to me that as Jesus said faith the size of a mustard seed could move mountains, and Thérèse counsels us to have desires and confidence the size of mountains, so we too have experience of mountains: these are the things we make out of molehills, the things that are just a little smaller (I'm imagining Mount Kilimanjaro or Everest) than our doubts and fears.

Forgive the cultural allusion, but in the words of Gene Wilder's Willy Wonka, "Strike that! Reverse it!" We've got it entirely backward, which is possibly why Thérèse doesn't slow down—if she were to wait for us, we might never catch up—but instead, repeats her mantra (to Jesus) "Draw me; we will run." She hears His voice, and before she takes off toward Him, she grabs the hands of anyone within reach and then *runs*!

Two who were near enough to grab during this period after her Act of Oblation were Céline, her sister and charge in the novitiate, and Marie of the Trinity, another of her novices. Céline was the sweet echo of her soul, and Thérèse had no hesitation in nabbing her. As she left the chapel on June 9, 1895, having just offered herself to Merciful Love, Thérèse grabbed Céline's hand and pulled her along to Mother Agnes, whose permission she then asked, stammering because she was so excited. Permission for what? For herself and Céline to offer themselves to Merciful Love. Mother Agnes, not knowing how important this was, instantly gave her consent.

I love Thérèse's "wise as a serpent" approach—she's in a hurry, better not to promote delay with long explanations or an air of intrigue; simultaneously simple as a dove she nabs Céline and immediately gains the permission. Only then does she tell Céline what this is about! Thérèse will write out an offering for the two of them to make as soon as possible. Sure enough, in two days she takes Céline before the statue of Mary which had been the instrument of many graces for their family, and Thérèse herself recites the prayer for both of them.

I am not a brilliant scholar. I do not (yet, to my sadness) even know French, let alone have access to the archives of Lisieux. (Actually, these are coming online in English, and at this writing are 85% available; nonetheless I am forever finding references to articles in *Vie Theresiennne*, the notebooks of Thérèse's sisters, etc., to which I have no access, even in French). I feel like Thérèse did—very little—and know, as she did, that this feeling reflects the truth. In other words, I am not and don't pretend to be an academic expert on Thérèse. (I've never wanted to be an academic expert on anything, but on St. Thérèse? That would be fun!)

I am, however, a girl with plenty of intuition and a long acquaintance with St. Thérèse and her writings (in English). A voracious collector of books and enthusiastic follower of rabbit trails (especially in Thérèse's world). But most of all, I have some measure of common sense, praise God.

When Jesus said, "I am the Bread of Life," and so on, as John recorded in the sixth chapter of his Gospel, He spoke plain as plain and meant what He said. When Thérèse prays, "Remain in me as in a tabernacle," she is being as clear, direct, and plain as Jesus. She means what she says, as He did.

And when I want to know what she meant—I mean really be sure, have every possible reassurance because this sounds crazy, outrageous, way too much—I go to her best friends.

It makes sense that St. John, the beloved disciple, the one who leaned on Jesus' breast at the Last Supper when Our Lord first gave Himself as food and drink in the Holy Eucharist, is also the one who tells us in no uncertain terms what Jesus said about the Blessed Sacrament. As he explained in his first letter, he and the other Apostles speak from first-hand experience of "what we have heard, what we have seen with our eyes, what we looked upon and touched with our hands" (1 John 1:1). He is a witness, a confidante, one who was there, so he's one I love to go to, one I can trust to tell me the most intimate secrets of Jesus' Heart.

And just as, when wanting to discover Jesus' riches, I can look to John and find the treasures God pours out to and through His best friends, so when seeking Thérèse's wealth, I can look to her closest disciples and find, again, the treasures God pours out to and through His friends.

When I want to learn about Jesus, the canonically approved books of Scripture will hold pride of place, and when I want to know more about Thérèse, after her writings, the Process takes pride of place. The friends of Thérèse were under oath when they testified, so their testimonies are, among all the accounts of her, most trustworthy. Later public documents written by her friends and close disciples—that is, the writings they intended for the public—then take precedence over their private correspondence. And all of their writings and sayings will be, without question, more important than the speculations of those who come later and comment upon them.

I bring this up now because we are asking a question with huge implications, and I want to make sure we get the answer right, and furthermore I want to do my best to convince little souls that this is true. If we operate under the great disadvantage of mountains of doubt which Thérèse would replace with mountains of confidence, let's give her all the help we can. This will require trusting her (so she can teach us to trust God). And trusting her has meant, from the get go, trusting those, too, in whom she put her confidence.

Céline, for one, Thérèse's own confidante and the soul-mate she immediately conscripted into the ranks of those (now two) making the Offering.

Pauline, whom Thérèse approached to gain permission, and to whom she gave *carte blanche* editorial freedom over her writings, particularly *Story of a Soul*.

Marie of the Sacred Heart, whom Thérèse next invited to make the Offering.

And finally Marie of the Trinity, whose witness, as we shall see, is singularly important.

First, then, Céline. She writes in *Memoir of My Sister, St. Thérèse* of the sequence of events beginning with Thérèse's inspiration during Mass on Trinity Sunday, "to make this *Act of Oblation to Merciful Love*." After Mass, Thérèse takes Céline with her to ask Mother Agnes' permission, then two days later, "Thérèse recited the Act of Oblation for both of us. Later on, the Saint communicated her secret to another novice, Sister Marie of the Trinity, and also to our eldest sister, Marie of the Sacred Heart" (*Memoir*, p. 90).

Certainly, then, Thérèse intended her Act of Oblation, and presumably everything it included, for some others. But Céline goes on to tell us, and the italicized emphasis is her own, "Then she wrote about it in her autobiography, and invited *all little souls* to share her riches."

There are at least two passages in *Story of a Soul* in which Thérèse indicates this universal invitation. First, in Chapter VIII (the end of Manuscript A); I will quote at length because this passage is key to understanding Thérèse's desires and intentions.

> This year, June 9, the feast of the Holy Trinity, I received the grace to understand more than ever before how much Jesus desires to be loved.
>
> I was thinking about the souls who offer themselves as victims of God's Justice in order to turn away the punishments reserved to sinners, drawing them upon themselves. This offering seemed great and very generous

to me, but I was far from feeling attracted to making it. From the depths of my heart, I cried out:

"O my God! Will Your Justice alone find souls willing to immolate themselves as victims? Does not Your *Merciful Love* need them too? On every side this love is unknown, rejected; those hearts upon whom You would lavish it turn to creatures, seeking happiness from them with their miserable affection; they do this instead of throwing themselves into Your arms and of accepting Your infinite *Love*, O my God! Is Your disdained Love going to remain closed up within Your Heart? It seems to me that if You were to find souls offering themselves as victims of holocaust to Your Love, You would consume them rapidly; it seems to me, too, that You would be happy not to hold back the waves of infinite tenderness within You. If Your Justice loves to release itself, this Justice *which extends only over the earth*, how much more does Your Merciful Love desire to set souls on *fire* since Your Mercy *reaches to the Heavens*. O my Jesus, let me be this happy victim; consume Your holocaust with the fire of Your Divine Love!" (pp. 180-181)

While Thérèse concludes by asking Jesus to let her be this happy victim, she has not limited her vision to herself alone. She has asked God, "Does not Your Merciful Love need them too?"—need, that is, souls willing to immolate themselves as victims. And again, she speaks of "souls offering themselves as victims of holocaust to Your Love"—"souls" in the plural, "victims" in the plural.

At the end of Chapter IX (Manuscript B), Thérèse's indication becomes more of a direct invitation. She is addressing God, and she is asking Him to share the grace of her oblation, and the many graces it called down upon her, with all little souls.

O Jesus! why can't I tell all *little souls* how unspeakable is Your condescension? I feel that if You found a soul weaker and littler than mine, which is impossible, You would be pleased to grant it still greater favors, provided it abandoned itself with total confidence to your infinite Mercy. But why do I desire to communicate Your secrets of Love, O Jesus, for was it not You alone who taught them to me, and can You not reveal them to others? Yes, I know it, and I beg You to do it. I beg You to cast Your Divine Glance upon a great number of *little* souls. I beg You to choose a legion of *little* Victims worthy of Your LOVE! (p. 200)

Her last line—"I beg You to choose a legion of little Victims worthy of Your LOVE!"—makes clear that St. Thérèse is again talking about the graces connected with her Offering to Merciful Love. Lest we immediately excuse ourselves, however, on the plea that while we are certainly little, we are certainly not "worthy," note that Marie of the Sacred Heart (at whose request Thérèse wrote Manuscript B) tried this before us, and Thérèse shed light on the question of "worthy."

In fact, turning to Thérèse's sister Marie, we find two indispensable aids to our understanding that Thérèse meant this offering for little souls like us. If Thérèse's lofty language sometimes makes us doubt its application to ourselves, we aren't the first. Marie wrote back in response to the passages we've quoted (which were originally given to her as a letter and reflection):

Dear little Sister … simply one word concerning myself. Like the young man in the Gospel, a certain feeling of sadness came over me in view of your extraordinary desires for martyrdom. That is the proof of your love; yes, you possess love, but I myself! No, never will you make me believe that I can attain this desired goal, for I dread all that you love. (*Letters of St. Thérèse of Lisieux*, Vol. II, p. 997)

Marie goes on to request, "I would like you to tell your little godmother, in writing, if she can love Jesus as you do."

We owe Marie so much! When we are sometimes afraid that Thérèse is in reality great, and not little, her sisters come to assure us that the complaint has been made already, and Thérèse always has an answer.

She replies to Marie, as requested, in writing:

My desires of martyrdom *are nothing*; they are not what give me the unlimited confidence that I feel in my heart. They are, to tell the truth, the spiritual riches that *render one unjust*, when one rests in them with complacence and when one believes they are *something great* ... These desires are a consolation that Jesus grants at times to weak souls like mine (and those souls are numerous), but when He does not give this *consolation*, it is a grace of *privilege* ... Dear Sister, how can you say after this that my desires are the sign of my love? ... Ah! I really feel that it is not this at all that pleases God in my little soul; what pleases Him is *that He sees me loving my littleness* and my *poverty, the blind hope that I have in His mercy* ... That is my only treasure, dear Godmother, why would this treasure not be yours? (*Letters*, Vol. II, p. 999; Letter 197)

Thérèse will not tolerate the false attribution of greatness to her small self. God alone is great; we are mere creatures and everything we have, we receive. Furthermore, she has constant proofs of her littleness—she is terrified of spiders, which makes her even worse at sweeping than she would have been due to no childhood training in domestic arts; she falls asleep constantly at prayer, her main "job" as a Carmelite; when the other nuns repeatedly praise her for her patience, she finally snaps and reiterates (but this time with real impatience) "I am not patient! It is God who can be virtuous within me!" Even as she begins, toward the end of her life, to prophetically know her future glory ("Save those, you'll need them," she says to the sister who has cut her fingernails, and "The whole world will love me!"), she is more sure than anything that what pleases God in her is nothing other than "the blind hope that I have in His mercy." And she asks us, as she asks Marie, "Why would not this treasure be yours?"

The Little Way is slightly more challenging—though always a relief, as Jesus' yoke is easy and light—than it might seem at first. Next time you say an idiotic thing and feel, not surprisingly, like an idiot, try to remember Thérèse's example. She said she was always doing this sort of thing (saying something foolish), but she would remember, along with "Ha! I'm right where I was before," to say gently to herself, "How good it is to be little!" because this gave God's infinite power great scope, just as He told St. Paul, "My power is perfected in weakness" (2 Corinthians 12: 8). Contrary to popular opinion, it's not about our being impressive. We get to be little and glorify God, whose love is so mighty and so merciful.

In the passages we've just quoted from *Story of a Soul,* Thérèse is talking to Marie about the offering they've both made. Their exchange of letters comes in September of 1896. We discover in Céline's *Memoir* that more than a year earlier, Thérèse had invited Marie to offer herself as a victim to Merciful Love. Let's look back at that incident, for Marie's response to Thérèse's invitation is another encouragement for little souls. Céline takes the following account from Sister Marie's infirmarian, who recorded (much later):

Today, June 6, 1934, I was speaking with Sister Marie of the Sacred Heart about the *Act of Oblation to Merciful*

Love. She told me she was raking the grass in the quadrangle one day in 1895 when Sister Thérèse, who was close by, asked if she would like to offer herself as a victim to the merciful love of God. "Indeed not," Sister Marie replied at once, "for if I offered myself as victim, God would take me at my word, and I have a great dread of suffering. Besides, far from inspiring me, the word *victim* has always repelled me."

Then Little Thérèse told her that she could well understand how she felt, but that to offer ourselves as victims to the Love of God is entirely different from giving ourselves over to His justice. It does not necessarily mean, she explained, an increase of suffering but merely the ability to love the good God more, and to make up for those souls who do not want to love Him. Thérèse's eloquence finally convinced her sister. "She won me over to her idea," Sister Marie said, "and I have never regretted having taken the step." (*Memoir*, pp. 90-91)

Céline expands on Thérèse's response to Marie by noting that Thérèse "always insisted that 'from this Oblation of self to God's love, we can expect mercy alone. We have nothing to fear from this Act,' she often exclaimed with holy ardour" (p. 92).

And what of Marie's offering? Céline tells us that Marie "proved to be one of the most ardent apostles of the Act of Oblation. She never hesitated to propose this Offering to her numerous correspondents, and, over that long period of years, she met with only one refusal, as far as I know" (*Memoir*, p. 91). Marie's last words when she died forty-five years after Thérèse talked her into making this offering were the words of the Act of Oblation.

Let's not get ahead of our story, though. At the time of her offering, Marie was as skeptical as we are about attaining the heights of Love. A year later—a year after she's made the offering—when Marie and her sister are exchanging letters in September of 1896, she still has fears precisely where Thérèse has noble desires, and she needs to know if there's a way for her to follow her saintly sister. Is there?

Thérèse continues in her reply to Marie's doubtful request:

> Oh, dear Sister, I beg you, understand your little girl, understand that to love Jesus, to be His *victim of love*, the weaker one is, without desires or virtues, the more suited one is for the workings of this consuming and transforming Love ... The *desire* alone to be a victim suffices, but we must consent to remain always poor and without strength, and this is the difficulty, for: "The truly poor in spirit, where do we find him? You must look for him from afar," said the psalmist ... He does not say that you must look for him among great souls, but "from afar," that is to say in *lowliness*, in *nothingness* ... Ah! let us remain then *very far* from all that sparkles, let us love our littleness, let us love to feel nothing, then we shall be poor in spirit, and Jesus will come to look for us, and *however far* we may be, He will transform us in flames of love ... Oh! How I would like to be able to make you understand what I feel! ... It is confidence and nothing but confidence that must lead us to Love .... Since we see the way, let us run together. Yes, I feel it, Jesus wills to give us the same graces, He wills to give us His Heaven *gratuitously*. (*Letters*, Vol. II, pp. 999-1000, Letter 197)

I am certain that Thérèse is sending us this same message and desiring with confidence that Jesus give us the same graces He gave her. Do we fit the qualifications? She's set them pretty low, but if we doubt we're good candidates, something will likely happen soon to re-convince of our littleness. As I heard a friend say, "I make my plans. I think, 'I can do this,' but I always forget what happens: I always forget the wrench that gets thrown into the works!" That wrench is so often our own inability, weakness, failure. We qualify, I promise.

Thérèse died very young, but she didn't think age had much to do with what matters. She realized God had given her a wisdom—His—beyond her years, and she longed to share it. Thanks to assignments given her by Mother Marie de Gonzague, Thérèse's zeal for God's message and love had an outlet: she taught the novices and wrote to two missionaries she had received as spiritual brothers. But even these positions of authority (relatively small though they were) had no effect on her estimation of her powers: it was all God, and many times He proved it, answering her prayers that He enlighten her charges when she was unable.

A few days before she died, Thérèse told Mother Agnes, "As far as little ones are concerned, they will be judged with great gentleness. And one can remain little, even in the most formidable offices, even when living for a long time. If I were to die at the age of eighty ... I would still die, I feel, as little as I am today" (*Last Conversations*, p. 199).

Littleness is the true size of the creature in comparison to the Creator. It is reality, fact, truth, no matter how "important" or "accomplished" or "successful" a person is. We are all very little souls (though I admit, for some of us, it's easier to see and accept). And Thérèse is inviting every one of us to the heights of union with God through her Act of Oblation.

Our question remains, though. Is she specifically inviting us to ask for the very unusual and seemingly extraordinary grace she asked for herself: the conservation of the Eucharist within us between Communions? Let us turn to another trustworthy source, the novice closest, after Céline, to Thérèse—Marie of the Trinity. She it is who holds the key.

Chapter 4

The Invaluable Witness of Marie of the Trinity

*She said it would be a disregard of the almighty power
and infinite goodness of God to restrain our desires
and hopes but, to the contrary, it would glorify Him
to nurture and increase them within ourselves.*

—Marie of the Trinity (Testimony in the Apostolic Process)

Marie of the Trinity was the third person (after Céline and Marie of the Sacred Heart) Thérèse asked to join in the Offering to Merciful Love. This Marie's first reaction was a joyful yes, but upon parting from Thérèse and thinking it over, she decided that since it was a serious offering, it deserved a serious preparation. She wasn't worthy, she wasn't ready; she would have to prepare in order to be more worthy, more ready.

Did I mention Thérèse is always in a hurry? She, like Jesus, is the same yesterday, today, and forever. She was in a hurry with Marie of the Trinity as with Céline and Marie of the Sacred Heart, and she is in a hurry now with us. God is waiting! Waiting for us to open ourselves to Him and receive His infinite tenderness; He's been extending the invitation for a long time—"Open wide your mouth and I will fill it"—but we are little and consequently slow. Thérèse wanted to be little and quick. So she told Marie of the Trinity, when this second Marie hesitated:

> Yes, this Act is even more important than we can imagine. But do you know what God requires of us by way of preparation? He requires us to admit our unworthiness. Since He has already given you this grace, give yourself up to Him without fear. Tomorrow morning after the thanksgiving, I will stay close to you in the oratory and while you make your Act, I will offer you to Jesus as the little victim that I have prepared for Him. (*Thérèse of Lisieux and Marie of the Trinity*, p. 87)

Marie of the Trinity did make her offering the next day, December 1, 1895, which she later called "that beautiful day, the most beautiful day of my life." And here is where her witness, her testimony, becomes invaluable to us.

We've made progress in our discussion of something new in St. Thérèse. We've discovered what that something new is, and we've established that, like all good ideas, it was God's idea first. We've seen that Thérèse has offered herself to Merciful Love, and that she's invited us to offer ourselves, too. We are now faced with the following questions:

Is Thérèse asking all little souls—that would include us—not only to make the Offering with her, but to ask for the particular graces for which she asks in the Act she wrote? Specifically, is she seriously inviting us to ask for a Eucharistic miracle, the conservation of the Sacred Species within us between Communions?

And if so, can we take her seriously? If she had these outrageous desires not only for herself, but also for us, can we go along with her? Does it make sense—again, is there any evidence—to desire a grace God seems to have reserved for only a few Saints, and Saints far advanced on the quest for holiness at that?

And finally, if we have the audacity to ask for this grace, is there reason to think God will grant it to the likes of us?

Marie of the Trinity answers all of these questions. Here is part of her testimony for the Apostolic Process, a Process requiring absolute and scrupulous honesty, under pain of perjury and excommunication. She testified:

> I was so flooded with graces on that beautiful day, the most beautiful day of my life, that all day long I experienced in a very tangible way the presence of the Eucharistic Jesus in my heart. I confided this to Sister Thérèse of the Child Jesus, who was not at all surprised and answered me simply:
>
> "Is God not omnipotent? If we so desire, it would not be difficult for Him to make His sacramental presence in our souls remain from one Communion to the next. Through this extraordinary feeling that you experienced today, He wishes to give you the pledge that all the requests you have made of him in the Act of Oblation will be lavishly granted. You will not always enjoy these feelings, but their effects will be no less real. One receives from God as much as one hopes for." (*Thérèse of Lisieux and Marie of the Trinity*, pp. 69-70)

(Let me note, parenthetically, something remarkable about Thérèse's words to Marie: They are strikingly similar to Jesus' words to Blessed Dina—words Thérèse couldn't have known because He uttered them decades later. Thérèse tells Marie: "Is God not omnipotent? If we so desire, it would not be difficult for Him to make His sacramental presence in our souls remain from one Communion to the next ... He wishes to give you the pledge that all the requests you have made of him in the

Act of Oblation will be lavishly granted." Jesus tells Blessed Dina: "My power and goodness are infinite. It is just as easy for Me to give Myself to you really by an intimate interior grace, invisible to all, as it is for Me to conceal Myself in the consecrated Host or in the chalice on the altar, under the appearance of wine ... I wish to lavish My graces upon you with prodigal generosity.")

We can draw from Marie's testimony the following points:

1. In response to Thérèse's invitation, with Thérèse's encouragement in advance and her assistance at the time of the offering, Marie prayed the full text of Thérèse's Act of Oblation to the Merciful Love of the Good God.

2. Marie then "experienced in a tangible way the presence of the Eucharistic Jesus" in her heart.

3. When Marie told Thérèse of her experience, Thérèse "was not at all surprised," and in simplicity explained to Marie that this confirmed God was pleased to answer the petitions of her Offering, which included the request for Jesus to "remain in me as in a tabernacle."

Father Descouvemont, the priest to whom I am indebted for making Marie's testimony available in his book *Thérèse of Lisieux and Marie of the Trinity*, adds in a footnote that Marie left another account of this same conversation with Thérèse.

Like Thérèse's sisters Céline (Sister Geneviève), Pauline (Mother Agnes), and Marie of the Sacred Heart, Marie of the Trinity would spend the rest of her life not only attempting to live the Little Way (as did, too, Thérèse's sister Léonie in her monastery of the Visitation at Caen), but also recording, compiling, and archiving every detail of life with Thérèse. Thus roughly forty years after her "most beautiful day," Marie of the Trinity was still reflecting on it. Here is her later account of what Thérèse had said to her:

This extraordinary feeling that you experience is proof that God lavishly grants all that you ask of Him. Yes, for His little 'victims of love,' He likes to make wondrous gifts which infinitely surpass their immense desires, but usually they labor in faith; otherwise they could not live. The Real Presence will not make itself felt, but it is no less existential. Nothing is impossible to the omnipotence of God and I am sure that He would not have inspired this request if He would not have wanted to realize it. (*Thérèse of Lisieux and Marie of the Trinity*, p. 70)

Let's pause here and take a deep breath.

I have read these two paragraphs—Marie's two accounts of Thérèse's words to her on the day of her Offering—numerous times. And really, I still can't get over them.

Here is what I love:

Marie of the Trinity is ordinary.

I haven't told much of her history, but she was younger than Thérèse and had come to the Lisieux Carmel after failing, due to poor health, at the Carmel in Paris, and there were doubts about whether she would make it in Lisieux.

Honestly, I love Marie of the Trinity. Like Céline and Marie of the Sacred Heart, she had a distinct and strong personality. Marie of the Sacred Heart was the independent one (who hated suffering!); Céline was the intrepid one (Thérèse had to continually remind her to detach herself from the work she was so determined to finish); and Marie of the Trinity was the passionate one. She was so distraught at Thérèse's approaching death that at times she couldn't control her weeping. Thérèse had a solution: she gave Marie a small shell into which she had to cry. Nothing like making a girl feel ridiculous to stop her taking life and death so seriously!

And I especially love Marie of the Trinity because where would we be without her testimony? We can always say about

Céline and Marie of the Sacred Heart: well sure, they may have been lesser Saints than Thérèse (who was, after all, "the greatest Saint of modern times" according to St. Pius X), but their parents are now officially canonized Saints, their sister Léonie has a process going, and from childhood they were constantly in company with Thérèse, who is hard sometimes to believe regarding her own littleness.

Marie of the Trinity didn't have these same advantages. She did grow up in a good Catholic home with excellent parents, but as far as I know no one has proposed her family for sainthood. In so many ways she's like the rest of us, only she had one special desire (Thérèse is so big on desires that this is an interesting side note): to sometime in her life be friends with a Saint. She desired a saint-friend like we might (if we thought of it), without necessarily thinking that God would grant her wish. But He did grant it, just as Thérèse said He always does—Marie and St. Thérèse became very close spiritual friends. And when Thérèse went to Heaven after they had lived in the monasetery together for only three years, Marie spent the rest of her life knowing Thérèse much the way we can—reflecting on her words (granted Marie had heard them personally) and trying to follow the Little Way.

In a letter to a friend, Marie wrote:

> My memories of Thérèse suffice me for my prayer and I know that God asks nothing other from me than to walk the 'Little Way' on which she guided my first steps. I do everything I can not to swerve from it; it is so easy to make a detour that you have to pay special attention in order to stay on it. But when I do, what peace! (*Thérèse and Marie*, p. 117)

I love that Marie swerved. That she found it so easy to make detours. That she had to pay special attention to stay on the Little Way. This reminds me of someone—me! But all the rest of us too, really, because you can find the same sentiments in the writings of Céline and Marie of the Sacred Heart. Here is one from Mother Agnes of Jesus, even: When asked in later years when she had made the Offering (have you noticed we haven't mentioned Thérèse's asking her? I think this is because of what Mother Agnes says next), she wouldn't give a direct reply. She said she was too embarrassed to tell because it took her a very long time to make her offering because it took so long for her to be convinced!

And yet, Mother Agnes became as staunch an advocate as any when she finally took the plunge. She wrote a postscript to one of Marie of the Trinity's letters to their correspondent from another Carmel, Sister Germaine:

> You have made me smile at the hesitation to the point of waiting until Christmas to surrender yourself to Love. Oh! Come on, there is nothing to fear because this way is a royal road and if we sometimes have a little fall, the Divine hand lifts us up immediately. Didn't our Mother Teresa [of Avila] say this in her time? And from the time of little Thérèse, which is ours, the way has been much enlarged to allow little souls like ours to pass. Yes, yes, we have everything that we need to become victims of Merciful Love, we have miseries to be consumed! What would Mercy do if it did not have to apply itself to our miseries?

At this point, my consideration always (for I have considered this many times) takes a leap upward in hope and confidence, and I'll tell you exactly why.

Having discovered that St. Thérèse had the outrageous idea of asking God to remain in her as in a tabernacle and that, wonderfully, God had the idea first, as we see in the lives of the Saints to whom He revealed that He had granted this grace (St. Anthony Mary Claret, St. Faustina, St. Padre Pio, St. Margaret Mary, Blessed

Dina Belanger); having further seen that Thérèse was confident God would grant her desires, and that she prayed God would give these desires to us too (and was confident He would grant our desires as well) ... I then think, "Okay, let's say God granted Thérèse this grace too. I've now got proof from five canonized Saints and one Blessed that God is happy to remain in them as in the tabernacle. What about those of us who are pretty ordinary? What reason do I have to think He wants to remain in us too?"

At this juncture, in walks Marie of the Trinity to fill me with hope. The good news? She doesn't have a cause in progress either. She is our ordinary one, at least she was very ordinary when Thérèse asked her to make the offering and assisted her in making it. And Thérèse was sure as ever—unsurprised as ever—when Marie told her that God seemed to be, well, remaining in her as in a tabernacle.

Which, as I've mentioned twice now, gives me tremendous hope. Because, to my chagrin, my husband recently informed me (not unkindly, but we had never had the conversation before) that there wouldn't be a cause for me after I die. Somehow, I'd been thinking all these years that sanctity equals canonized sanctity, even though I've known any number of holy people who are surely in Heaven if God is true (and He is), though they'll likely never have causes. But now, with Marie of the Trinity before me, I've decided I don't need a cause, I don't need to die recognizably holier-than-thou—I, too, can keep getting back on the Little Way when I fall off, and I can, in virtue of following it, by definition really, expect to live an intimacy with God beyond most of the canonized Saints' wildest expectations.

I can also, according to Thérèse, expect God to fulfill all my desires, and according to her novice and invaluable witness, Marie of the Trinity, I can expect, moreover, to receive the grace of the Eucharistic Jesus' Real Presence abiding within me between Communions.

As to God fulfilling all my desires, here is a proof I received which leads to more of Marie's convincing testimony.

I had, for many years, a kind of daydream in which I made a pilgrimage to Lisieux and found myself in the archives of Thérèse's Carmel, where her sisters (those of the present day) gave me some erstwhile unknown manuscripts from which I would mine Thérésian treasures. In more vivid versions of this daydream, the archivist placed into my eager hands the notebooks of Marie of the Trinity.

In an entirely unexpected way, the pilgrimage I dreamed of actually occurred. My husband and I traveled to Lisieux, and although I didn't make it into the archives of the Carmel nor meet any of Thérèse's Carmelite sisters, our visit did facilitate one of my deepest desires: through the kindness of two of Thérèse's sweet devotees and employees, I obtained copies of certain of Marie of the Trinity's notebooks as reprinted in old issues of *Vie Thérésienne* (Thérésian Life). These were the notebooks from which Fr. Descouvement had drawn his pages on Marie of the Trinity and her Offering to Merciful Love; these were essential, too, for the work of that magnificent friend of St. Thérèse, Bishop Guy Gaucher, who wrote in his book *John and Thérèse: Flames of Love*, "The publication of her [Marie's] notebooks in *Vie Thérésienne* constitutes a source of great value that has scarcely been exploited until now."

I'm delighted to exploit these notebooks for our purposes, for they have fulfilled not only my first desire (of finding them), but also my second and more important longstanding desire: As I had hoped, in them Marie gives new details of her own experience, she argues convincingly for the reality of Jesus' remaining within us between Communions, and she even addresses the objection that this is a crazy desire and request.

Taking the last first, Marie addresses, albeit indirectly, the concern that Thérèse has finally gone too far with this petition.

In her testimony before the tribunal, Marie states plainly regarding Thérèse's virtue of hope:

> It is impossible to push it further than she did. She loved to repeat "that one obtains from God as much as one hopes for." She told me that she felt in herself infinite desires to love the good God, to glorify Him and to make Him loved and that she firmly hoped that her desires would all be realized and more! She said that it was to deny the omnipotence and infinite goodness of God to restrain these desires and hopes, but on the contrary it was to glorify Him to develop them in oneself. "I would pass for insane," she said to me, "if I were to enumerate all I hope of the good God!"

As for the new details of her own experience, in passages similar to the ones we have quoted above, Marie gives us a much fuller picture of the emotions and consolations she and Thérèse experienced. Here is Marie's account, which I have combined from two of her recollections:

> We decided that I would make the Act the first Sunday of Advent, 1895. It was the 30th of November that St. Thérèse of the Child Jesus made me know the Act of Offering to Love. Her words were so convincing and passionate that a great desire was born in me to imitate her and it was agreed between us that I would make the same Act the next day. However, I remained alone, and reflecting on my unworthiness, I concluded that I needed a longer preparation … I was so seized by the grandeur of the Act that I was going to make, that I said to Sister Thérèse of the Child Jesus that I did not feel well enough prepared, and that a victim so imperfect as me could not be approved by Jesus with pleasure. Immediately her

face became radiant with happiness, and hugging me, she told me:

"I was afraid you did not understand the importance of the Act which I am having you make; what you tell me confirms the opposite. How happy I am! Do not be afraid, Jesus will receive you tomorrow with joy and love, it is enough for you to recognize your unworthiness for Him to do great things in you ..."

The next day everything went well. But how to describe the abundance of consolations that inundated our souls? I felt so overwhelmed under the weight of the Divine Mercy that it seemed to me my heart was going to break, I was likely to die of love. And when, leaving the Chapel, we wanted to share our feelings, we couldn't do it except by our tears ...

How intense this experience of the Act was for Marie and Thérèse! But returning to our essential question, we must still ask: Had Jesus actually consented to remain in Thérèse, and later in Marie, and will He now consent to remain in us, as in so many tabernacles housing His abiding Real Presence between our receptions of Holy Communion?

Fortunately, we aren't the first to ask. I discovered in *Vie Thérésienne* that Sister Germaine Leconte of the Carmel of Angers had the same concerns a century ago, along with the advantage of a correspondence with Thérèse's little novice and protégée Marie of the Trinity. And happily, in her letter to Sister Germaine on January 3, 1911, Marie answers all of our questions in words as clear as they are compelling. Taking the letter part by part, we find first Marie's argument for Thérèse's experience:

I remember that I promised you certain details about the opinion that we have that the Eucharistic Jesus dwelt continually in the soul of our little saint. For me it is my intimate conviction, because would it be the only desire that Jesus had not realized for her? I cannot believe it, she begged for it each day with such ardour! Then, a fact which is personal to me confirms in me the assurance of her possessing such a favor. I wish to recount it to you in all simplicity.

Next, in words we have seen before but are well worth revisiting, Marie relates her own experience and Thérèse's assurance of its meaning, which answers our question about whether Marie herself actually retained the Eucharistic Jesus in her soul between Communions. She continues in her letter to Sister Germaine:

> The day when I offered myself as a victim of holocaust to the Merciful Love of the good God, 1st of December, 1895, I was so inundated with graces on this beautiful day, the most beautiful of my life, that all day I felt in a sensible manner the presence of Jesus-Host in my heart. I confided this to Sister Thérèse of the Child Jesus who appeared not at all surprised and responded simply:
> "The good God, is He not All-Powerful? It is not difficult for Him, according to our desire, to make His sacramental presence subsist in our souls from one communion to the other. By this extraordinary feeling that you experienced today, He wants to give you the pledge that all the requests that you have made of Him in the Act of offering will be magnificently granted. You will not always enjoy this feeling but the effects will be no less real. One receives from God as much as one hopes for."

We have seen so far in this letter Marie's argument for the Eucharistic Jesus remaining in Thérèse between Communions, and Thérèse's argument for Jesus' Real Presence remaining in Marie between Communions. Finally, in the remaining portion of Marie's letter to Sister Germaine, we will find the sequel to Marie's "extraordinary feeling" on the day she initially made her offering, and her wonderful conclusion which addressed not only what she thought of her own experience, but what she holds regarding ours:

> In fact, I have never again felt this sweet grace of 1st December 1895 but this does not alter the fact that despite the aridities, the life of faith that I lead, I preserve the certitude that the Eucharistic Jesus resides constantly in my heart and that this marvelous grace is the portion of all the little victims of love. If it were not so, what good would it do each day to make this request when one is sure in advance of not having it realized? It would be useless! All that I ask, I think that the good God gives me and this thought dilates my soul, collects it, does it good. If I am deceived (which I do not believe) well, my error has served to unite me more to Jesus and I do not regret it.

In a note written around 1935, nearly twenty-five years after this letter to Sister Germaine, Marie has not forgotten what she experienced and how Thérèse responded. Nor has Thérèse's former novice, now a fully professed sixty-year-old nun, changed her firm opinion. Writing again about her "day from Heaven," she recollects:

> I have never had in all my life so many spiritual consolations, I was likely to die of love. I made my Act of offering, with the conviction of being granted all my requests and all day I felt the Real Presence of the Sacred Host in my heart. Sister Thérèse of the Child Jesus, to whom I confided my impressions, appeared not at all surprised, she herself tasted a celestial happiness and her tears of love mingled with mine ...

Marie goes on to recall once again Thérèse's assurance:

This extraordinary feeling that you experience is a proof that the good God will magnificently grant all you ask. Yes, for the little victims of love, He is pleased to do marvels that infinitely surpass their immense desires, but usually they operate in faith, otherwise they could not live. The Real Presence will not make itself felt, but it exists nonetheless. Nothing is impossible to the omnipotence of God and I am sure that He would not have inspired this request, if He hadn't wanted to fulfill it.

Marie had written to Sister Germaine in 1911, "I preserve the certitude that the Eucharistic Jesus resides constantly in my heart and that this marvelous grace is the portion of all the little victims of love." In conclusion to this note of 1935, she repeats her answer to the question at the heart of this book: Even if we grant that the Real Presence has remained sacramentally in some of the greatest Saints between Communions, can we too, truly little souls, ask and expect from Jesus this remarkable Eucharistic grace? With decades of religious life behind her, Marie of the Trinity tells us simply:

For me, this grace, more extraordinary it is true than ecstasies, visions, or revelations, can be the lot of little souls, without taking them out of their little way of humility, since it is a grace granted to their humble confidence and which operates in bare faith, therefore safe from pride and vainglory.

Thérèse one day repeated "with an air of conviction" a line from a holy book, *Petits Fleurs*, "The Saints of the latter days will surpass those of the first days just as the cedars surpass the other trees" (*Last Conversations*, p. 101). Which might help us to accept the outrageous idea that God intends to give us this extraordinary grace. This reminds me of the first "Saying of Light and Love" of her holy Father in Carmel, St. John of the Cross. He tells us, "The Lord has always revealed to men the treasures of His wisdom and His spirit, but now that the face of evil more and more bares itself, so does the Lord bare His treasures the more."

Perhaps we shouldn't be surprised that God has such infinite love and longing for us. He sent His beloved Son to suffer for us and die on the cross that He might rise (in a body like ours, though His was now glorified) to save us from eternal death. Then He promised to stay with us always until the end of time, which He does in the Holy Eucharist. All of which, the theologians tell us, gained Him nothing, since He already has or is everything.

But what are we to think about this newest expression of His love, this latest treasure of His Wisdom and His Spirit, this favor I'm convinced His littlest Apostle, Thérèse, is in a mad rush to convert us to desiring and requesting?

Let us think what she thinks. We cannot do better than think the thoughts of one who pleased Him so well, gained all the desires of her heart, and is distinguished by the doctorate of the Church. She is in the same quandary we are: she knows God needs nothing, and yet—and yet, as she tells us in *Story of a Soul*, "The same God who declares *He has no need to tell us when He is hungry* did not fear *to beg* for a little water from the Samaritan woman. He was thirsty. But when He said: '*Give me to drink*,' it was the *love* of His poor creature the Creator of the universe was seeking. He was thirsty for love" (p. 189).

The answer, it would seem, is to let Him drink freely by letting Him remain in us. As in a tabernacle? That is certainly the idea, but first, we have more objections to overcome.

Chapter 5

Replies to Further Objections

No, no, let us not listen to the demon, who represents to us our desires and efforts as so many acts of pride, as vain attempts to imitate the Saints! For how advantageous it is to the soul to excite itself thus to great things! In fact, even if at the moment it has not strength to realize its pious ambitions, it has at least aroused a generous impulse, and nothing remains but to march forward.

—St. Teresa of Avila

Not to be a wet blanket, but as I attempt to go from believing in this grace of Love to asking for it myself, more objections keep crowding in. I wouldn't be surprised if many of them are from the devil, but I also wouldn't be surprised if many were simply excuses from my own timid soul, or to take a less dim view, the cavils of common sense. No matter their origin, let's examine these further objections so we may lay them to rest too.

Objection 1: Are we saying the Act is a kind of magic formula by which we can "force" Jesus to remain in us?

This is an important objection because St. Thérèse's logic of love can be so compelling that we may think we have only to parrot her words to get every good thing. Alas, unlike parrots, we will have to put our human hearts into this prayer if we want to truly appeal to Jesus.

In the "Counsels and Reminiscences" that accompanied early editions of *Story of a Soul*, one of Thérèse's novices tells us that she asked Thérèse something like this very question. After Thérèse had told of one of the fruits of the Act, the novice said, "To enjoy such a privilege, would it suffice to repeat that Act of Oblation which you have composed?" Thérèse replied, "Oh, no! words do not suffice. To be a true Victim of Love we must surrender ourselves entirely ... *Love will consume us only in the measure of our self-surrender.*"

Thérèse's answer is reminiscent of the passage from *Story of a Soul* where she tells Jesus, "I feel that if You found a soul weaker and littler than mine, which is impossible, You would be pleased to grant it still greater favors, provided it abandoned itself with total confidence to Your Infinite Mercy." Which leads us to our next objection.

Objection 2: We have no problem fulfilling Thérèse's condition that our souls be weaker and littler than hers, but if she's setting as further conditions that we "must surrender ourselves entirely" and "abandon ourselves with total confidence" to God's infinite Mercy, isn't the game up?

I think this objection is straight from the devil because it has such a slippery, slimy, totally unanswerable feel to it. We, however, are on God's side, and His Truth easily vanquishes the devil's lies.

I admit that "complete surrender" and "abandonment with total confidence"—and these are Thérèse's requirements—sound absolutely beyond our reach. But let's think before we panic. Is it a daily flogging Thérèse suggests? Fasting on moldy bread and stagnant water? Leaving our families and entering a convent or monastery? Never saying a sharp word?

Thérèse is requiring none of these. We might think the last one, at least, would be part of her Little Way. Well sure, gentleness is optimal, but Thérèse is a realist; she knows we'll fall frequently, if not constantly. So what she asks—what she *requires*, or rather what she's learned that God requires—is more basic, more in keeping with our littleness: to surrender to Him who is Love; to abandon ourselves with confidence into the arms of our loving Father. These two conditions are really the same, and they are her constant theme. In Chapter IX of *Story of a Soul*, for instance, she writes:

> I understand so well that it is only love that makes us acceptable to God, that this love is the only good I ambition. Jesus deigned to show me the road that leads to this Divine Furnace, and this road is the *surrender* of the little child who sleeps without fear in its Father's arms. (p. 188)

Thérèse's goal is union with God, and her game plan can be summed up in a description used to sum up the first three steps of the famous twelve steps of Alcoholics Anonymous: "We can't. He can. Let Him." This surrender can be both easier and harder than anything we've ever done. But it isn't an elusive or impossible requirement Thérèse is making up, and if it were truly difficult, she'd know it was beyond little souls. When you come down to it, it's a blessed relief.

To pray the Act and mean it, we will need to spend time thinking about who God is and who we are. I recommend putting the emphasis on who God is. He is Love, and the more we understand what that means and believe it, the more natural and habitual our surrender to Him will become.

Objection 3: If, like Thérèse did and urges us to do, we ask Jesus to remain with us as in a tabernacle, aren't we inviting Him to stay in us only to be ignored? What about our inability to remain with Him?

I've thought about this objection a lot because I really want to live this Eucharistic grace, but I know myself and I'm terrible at paying attention for the fifteen minutes after Communion when I know Jesus is remaining with me—let alone any longer than that. St. Thérèse said that in her life she hadn't gone three minutes without thinking of God; in my life I doubt I've ever gone three minutes thinking of God!

Nonetheless, I have several replies to this objection and I fancy they come directly from my guardian angel, good and faithful friend that he is.

First, we have two examples to illustrate that the ability to remain recollected is not the condition of this miracle. In the case of Marie of the Trinity, let's recall Thérèse's words to her very normal (not at the height of sanctity) novice:

> Yes, this Act is even more important than we can imagine. But do you know what God requires of us by way of preparation? He requires us to admit our unworthiness. Since He has already given you this grace, give yourself up to Him without fear. (*Thérèse of Lisieux and Marie of the Trinity*, p. 87)

Thérèse did convince Marie to make the offering the next day, during their thanksgiving after Holy Mass. These were women following a daily *horarium*, and after Marie made the Act, they would have left the chapel and proceeded with the rest of their day.

Even the position of the petition within the Act itself would argue against the kind of baseline attention we know such a petition deserves. But God's ways are not our ways, and Marie would have had to make her petition for Jesus to remain with her and move along in the prayer in order to recite the whole and complete her offering.

When assailed by the knowledge of my own lack of recollection, I am delighted to remember that thanks to Marie of the Trinity's hesitation, Thérèse once had the perfect opportunity to name any requirements she chose for her candidates for the Act. In her compassion for God's thirst for us, she named only one: our recognition that we are unworthy—which can include our acknowledgement that we will be poor company for the King of Heaven, but when we recall that He is the one who is thirsting, how can we deny Him the drink of our love that is His only satiety?

I also find comfort in St. Anthony Mary Claret's account of his reception of this grace. He wrote, "I now bear within me day and night the adorable Eucharist. I must therefore be always recollected and cultivate the interior life." Unlike the novice Marie of the Trinity when she made the Offering and felt the physical presence of Christ (which Thérèse interpreted as a sign that God was answering her petition), St. Anthony Mary Claret was, when he received this grace, already well advanced in the spiritual life and union with God. And yet, his reaction was not, "Thank goodness I've got such an excellent habit of continual recollection," but rather, "Egads, I'd better get really focused now!"

Jesus, in other words, does not wait for us to be already perfectly united to Him before He comes to us. Perhaps even He cannot wait that long! Or rather, the wait would be fruitless since it is His own Presence which will teach us to love Him. This is an important point we will return to at the end of this chapter. And if, meanwhile, you think you cannot possibly begin to be recollected like St. Anthony Mary Claret was before he received this grace, let alone after, join the club. Again, Thérèse had her chance to name any condition she chose for our readiness to make the Act. It was only to acknowledge our unworthiness, not to be (or even become) champions of the long attention span.

My second reply regarding our lack of recollection is that we will not leave Him any more alone within us than He is already so often left alone in most of the tabernacles of the world.

My third reply, and this is where I especially see the inspiration of my guardian angel, is that we do not have to fear leaving Jesus alone in us, because since we are taking Him with us everywhere, and since our guardian angels always accompany us by God's express command, we can be confident that our guardian angels will make up for our deficiency in the proper adoration of God within us. As the hymn "Praise My Soul the King of Heaven" expresses it, our prayer can be, "Angels help us to adore Him, you behold Him face to face."

In sum, while this objection may spring from self-knowledge, the devil has a hand in frequently reminding us of our shortcomings in such a way that they disturb our peace. We have another angel to help us combat him, and this good guardian is also the one who can help us overcome our fear of leaving Christ lonely within us. Not only will our angel remind us to abandon our poor selves to Jesus with trust in His love; he will also supply what we lack even while he teaches us how to pray.

But there is more. It helps tremendously to realize that, as we saw with Anthony Mary Claret, even the greatest Saints are aware of their pitiful attention spans. In her *Spiritual Testimonies*, St. Teresa of Avila tells us, "On the Tuesday following Ascension Thursday, having remained a while in prayer after Communion, I was grieved because I was so distracted I couldn't concentrate. So I complained to the Lord about our miserable nature" (*St. Teresa of Avila, Collected Works,* ICS, Vol. I, p. 391).

Here is a Saint who has often experienced enormous favors from the Lord, including visions, raptures, and locutions. More importantly, she has been accompanying Him daily in her prayer life for decades by this time. Yet how human she is! We must take our cues from the Saints and not be too hard on ourselves, but aware as they are of our frailty and poverty, let us with them complain to the Lord about our miserable nature. See how Teresa doesn't allow her distraction to draw her away from Christ, but as soon as she is aware of it, it becomes, like everything else, a means of drawing her toward Him, or better yet of drawing Him to her. He is within her. Her mind and heart wander. She complains to Him!

Thérèse with her recurrent, if unintentional, napping after Holy Communion, knew this challenge of attending to the Lord even at the moments we are most certain of His physical presence within us. What is her perspective on recollection (and lack thereof)? A true daughter of her holy Mother in Carmel, little Thérèse first acknowledges the misery of our human nature, but like the big Teresa, she doesn't expect that to stop God's advances. Céline writes in her *Memoir*:

> "If God should desire beautiful thoughts and sublime sentiments," she used to say, "He has His angels! Furthermore, He could have created human beings already perfect with none of the weaknesses of our nature. But no; He finds His delight in poor little weak and miserable creatures, like ourselves. Evidently, He derives greater pleasure from this choice." (p. 32)

In a similar vein, Fr. Francoise Jamart, when speaking of Thérèse's simplicity, relates:

> One of her companions complained because she was not able to direct her will often to God. Thérèse reassured her: "That 'direction' is not necessary for those who are entirely dedicated to our Lord. No doubt, it is a good

thing to recollect our mind, but we should do that gently, for constraint does not glorify the good Lord. He is well acquainted with the nice thoughts and the elegant expressions of love which we would like to address to him, but He is satisfied with our desires. Is He not our Father and are we not His little children?" (*Complete Spiritual Doctrine of St. Thérèse of Lisieux*, p. 120)

We find here a caveat. Thérèse tells us we need not worry about our lack of recollection if we are "entirely dedicated to our Lord." But wait—don't throw in the towel! Thérèse is merely singing her usual refrain, albeit this time with slightly different words. To be "entirely dedicated" is the natural consequence of our realization that God is our Father and we are His little children. It is, again as always with Thérèse, simply our surrender that Jesus requires. Don't worry if surrender seems as elusive as the "nice thoughts," "elegant expressions," and the sustained attention we would like to but constantly fail to give Him. We'll say more about this surrender in the next chapters.

Objection 4: Just before asking Jesus to remain in her as in a tabernacle, St. Thérèse insists that the more God wants to give us, the more He makes us desire. But don't we have all kinds of desires that God doesn't fulfill? How can we know this desire is really from Him?

This is a powerful objection because it strikes at the heart of Thérèse's argument for attaining this Eucharistic grace. As with so many other things she's asked for, she's confident of obtaining this gift from God because she is convinced He wants to give it to her. Marie of the Trinity confirms, "She told me that He would not have inspired this request if He had not wanted it to be realized." Thérèse also said, "God is so mighty and so merciful; one obtains from Him as much as one hopes for." We have, then, two problems. First, how do we know that God has inspired this prayer; and second, even if He is behind it, why does that mean He will fulfill it?

Let's note before anything else that St. Thérèse is not making up this principle, but getting it straight from another Doctor of the Church, St. John of the Cross. And lest we worry that she misunderstands his doctrine, takes it out of context, or uses it erroneously, we have no less an authority than Blessed Father Marie-Eugene of the Child Jesus (a master of Carmelite doctrine and Definitor General of the Order) telling us about Thérèse: "She is the only one, we could say, to have read and perfectly understood St. John of the Cross" (*Under the Torrent of His Love*, p. 32).

Then what about this principle she borrows from him? St. John of the Cross taught, long before she repeated him, "The more God wants to give us, the more He increases our desires, even making the soul empty so that He can refill it with His goods" (Letter to Madre Leonor de San Gabriel, July 9, 1589).

St. Thérèse loved this saying because it increased her hope and confidence, and as time passed, she could see its truth more and more in her life. Around the time of Mother Teresa of Calcutta's canonization, I read something similar about her—that she had great trust in God's providence and ability to provide, and while at first her trust was simply a result of her faith, as time went on, as the decades passed and God always came to her assistance in very practical ways (repeatedly providing food for the hungry, and so much more, through her, though she was utterly poor), her experience almost rendered her faith in God's providence unnecessary. She could simply say, "I know He will do it because I have seen Him do it every time."

So too, Thérèse began by trusting this dictum because it came from her holy Father in Carmel, St. John of the Cross. But as time went on, what seemed reasonable became simply obvious. She, like us, had any number of desires, and they ranged, like

ours do, from the frivolous to the sublime. She carefully noted
that God fulfilled them all.

She wanted to be freed from various impediments that
blocked her experience of God's love, in particular her childhood hypersensitivity and her scruples; He freed her from them.
She desired and prayed and sacrificed for the conversion of a
murderer, a man named Pranzini, and she asked God for a sign
that he would converted before he was executed—she wanted a
sign just this once, so she would be encouraged, but she assured
God she would trust that He had granted her real desire (for the
conversion) even without the sign. God gave her the conversion
and the sign.

She wanted to enter the Carmel at fifteen; after giving her
the gift of waiting for a few months beyond her fifteenth birth-
day, God granted her desire. She wanted snow on her clothing
day (surely a desire more worthy of a child than a Saint?); He
provided it, as He alone could do. She wanted with all her heart
for Céline to enter the Carmel, though it seemed impossible;
God removed all obstacles and her wish came true.

I think it's fair to guess that Thérèse may have had desires she
didn't tell us about, desires that weren't fulfilled. But if so, it's also
fair to guess that she remained silent on that front because they
were desires not worthy of the name, desires she had decided
were not from God, and therefore not "inspired by Him so He
could fulfill them."

Speaking for myself, I certainly have many desires that remain
unfulfilled. But if I'm allowed a distinction, I would say these unfulfilled desires are of three kinds. First, those that aren't worthy
of the name because they don't persist. Second, the kind God
hasn't answered yet, but will. And third, those that He answers in
a more creative way than I had originally requested or imagined.

In the first category are my desires that come and go. Last
week I wanted a puppy. (I'm not kidding, and yet Thérèse's desire

for snow helps me keep a straight face as I reveal my pantheon of childish—or childlike—desires.) Then I happened to visit a friend who had a new puppy. Sweet as my friend's puppy was, I went home cured of my "desire" and thanking God that He hadn't rushed to fulfill my request. I'm guessing Thérèse had wishes like this too, but knew them more for whims which don't quite qualify as bona fide desires.

[Since writing the preceding paragraph, I discovered that my example was not the best for this first category of desires. Not only did the desire for a puppy return to my heart, but eventually a puppy materialized in our home. Nonetheless, the category still stands, though the example broke through to our next playing field.]

In the second category I would place my fervent and persistent desire for the return to the Faith of those who have left it. I am confident this desire is inspired by God, and yet I must remember that "Love is patient." He is patient, and I must be too, knowing that He will wait for the right moment to fulfill my desire as it pertains to each particular soul. Thérèse also had to wait and didn't always see a sign like the one God gave her in the case of her "first-born," Pranzini. This is where confidence comes in, and patience: confidence in His infinitely powerful love and mercy, patience with His timing which is always better than ours.

In the third category, I could put my desire for a large family. I had thought that God would fulfill that desire by giving me many children. In a much more creative fashion than I could have foreseen, He's given me two children born twelve years apart. A large family indeed when considered in terms of years-in-the-nest!

For Thérèse, God answered her many conflicting desires (for martyrdom—by every means, for missionary work—in every corner of the globe, etc.) by making her Love in the Heart of the Church. After her entrance into eternal life, He's continued answering her desires—we might think some of these desires fall into category two, such as her desire to be a Doctor of the Church (for that one, she had to wait a little while). Others, most especially her desire of doing good after her death by showering roses from Heaven and coming down, are definitely category three. God has granted these desires in abundantly various and marvelous ways—more creative ways than even she could have imagined, as the volumes of "Showers of Roses" kept by the Lisieux Carmel attest.

Objection 5: What if I don't have this desire?

Thérèse herself admitted to a desire she didn't have: she had no desire to offer herself as a Victim to God's Justice. The circumstances of her noting this "missing" desire are interesting. Nothing is vague with Thérèse, and it was at a specific time and for a specific reason that she discovered her lack of desire (I think we could put it more strongly and call it her aversion) to offer herself to Justice.

In the refectory of her monastery Thérèse heard, read aloud, the obituary notice of a nun from another Carmel. Such a notice was the custom, and it explains how *Story of a Soul* came to be printed: when a Carmelite nun died, the monastery would put together a circular letter telling of the life and virtues of the nun who had died, to send to the other Carmels for their edification and to ask for their prayers. In Thérèse's case, Mother Agnes gathered her little sister's memoirs into *Story of a Soul* to send to the other Carmels. But in the case of this poor nun, who died two years before Thérèse did, the letter was not so long, and not anywhere near as encouraging.

The story read in the refectory was about how this deceased nun had offered herself as a victim to Divine Justice, and you could say it *did* inspire Thérèse—to make a different kind of offering. Here is what she tells us in Chapter VIII of *Story of a Soul*:

I was thinking about the souls who offer themselves as victims of God's Justice in order to turn away the punishments reserved to sinners, drawing them upon themselves. This offering seemed great and very generous to me, but I was far from feeling attracted to making it. (p. 180)

She goes on to explain how she thought God's Love was much more in need of victims than was His Justice. And so on Trinity Sunday, the day after that circular was read, Thérèse responded to her desire to be a victim of Love with her own offering.

What inspires me here, besides Thérèse's explanation of how her own offering will work, is her large-souled response to the other nun's offering. "This offering seemed very generous to me," she writes, although she "was far from feeling attracted to making it."

I get this. I mean I really get not wanting to offer myself to Justice, but I can also relate to St. Thérèse seeing someone else's desire as generous without in any way sharing that desire.

In her testimony, Mother Agnes highlighted two of Thérèse's desires as expressed in the Act of Oblation. Along with the request that Jesus remain in her as in a tabernacle, she had another unusual petition. Thérèse asked to bear the wounds of Christ in her glorified body in Heaven.

When I first read that, and for decades thereafter, I was far from feeling attracted to asking for this second particular grace. Especially because, to my dismay, Thérèse works up to the petition by praying, "I thank You, O my God! for all the graces You have granted me, especially the grace of making me pass through the crucible of suffering."

Very generous, but I don't think so, Thérèse.

For a very long time I was unable to repeat her "Thank You especially for the grace of suffering," but no matter, I just let my mind wander while I read that paragraph. God and I understood we had a deal: I wasn't super grateful for suffering, and He didn't have to grant me, in Heaven, the grace of bearing His stigmata in my glorified body.

I'm still not in love with suffering, but I've come a little closer to being grateful for all He's given me, including the suffering (at least the suffering that's in the past. I manage to hope against hope that the future will be without this gift). So now I don't mind reciting this paragraph with Thérèse, though most often I say the Act from the beginning to the part about "Remain in me as in a tabernacle," and stay with that petition for a while, then jump down to the offering itself, skipping the entirety of the intervening paragraphs.

I like to think Thérèse would approve, and advise us, "Pray as you can, not as you ought."

But I have to confess something else: I wasn't particularly interested in the petition for Jesus to "remain in me," either, until this past year. I don't recall it bothering me, but the Act of Oblation is quite a long prayer, and if you skip parts, there's still plenty left to say to God. So much so that when Thérèse's sisters requested the Vatican to attach indulgences to the Act, the Holy See responded by attaching them to the part of the Act that begins, "In order to live in one single act of perfect Love, I offer myself…" That is, the Holy See added indulgences especially to the last three paragraphs, the first of which we might call the "offering proper." That's the part that especially attracted me, and I didn't worry about the rest.

Now, as you can see, I'm quite taken with Thérèse's request for Jesus to remain in me as in a tabernacle, but I know this is not an inspiration universally shared—at least not yet.

While in the process of writing this book, I confided its subject to two dear friends, both little souls, and both greatly in love with Jesus. They both had the same reaction: "You're writing a book on Thérèse? Finally!" and then when I told them, somewhat shyly, the particular topic, they had a different reaction (different from their first response, but still the same as each other) and their reaction is slightly reminiscent of how Thérèse felt in another context. They thought it was a generous idea (this invitation for Jesus to remain in us sacramentally between Communions), but it was not an idea to which they themselves felt attracted.

Like Thérèse, I have no inclination to recruit souls to offer themselves to God's justice, but I do desire, with her, to help little souls experience more of God's love. She has taught me to see the Act of Offering to His Merciful Love, and especially the request that He remain in us as in a tabernacle, as perfect ways to invite His infinite tenderness into our hearts. If you don't yet have a desire to make the Offering, or if you don't yet have this desire for Him to remain in you as in a tabernacle, our hope is that this book will plant the seeds.

Time has passed since I initially broached the subject with my two friends, we continued to discuss Jesus' crazy desire, and a third friend became involved in the conversations. What I've noticed is that while my friends have come to see the unquestionable truth of Jesus' "something new" in St. Thérèse, they continue to encounter obstacles to experiencing this desire themselves. The biggest obstacle to their desire relates, however, to the question of recollection, which we considered in Objection 3, and which we can now rephrase as: How can we ask Jesus to remain in us if we have no desire to radically change our lives in order to remain in Him?

This combination of our current objection (what if I don't desire this grace?) and the earlier one (how can I ask if I can't stay recollected in Him?) is powerful enough to merit its own answer, so let's address it next.

Objection 6: How can we ask Jesus to remain in us if we have no desire to radically change our lives in order to remain with Him in us?

This objection arises from a misunderstanding of what Jesus expects from us. In particular, I've found that the quotation from St. Anthony Mary Claret about his need for deeper and more continuous recollection after he had received this grace, while intended to reassure us that even the greatest Saints aren't perfect, has more effectively frightened the daylights (or the desire to ask Jesus to remain in them as in a tabernacle) out of my friends. Oops!

Let me try again.

The beauty of this petition for Jesus to remain in us as in a tabernacle is not only that it's asking for a union with Jesus that will satisfy the desires of His Heart and satiate His thirst, but ours as well.

If we were holier, perhaps satisfying Jesus (and not ourselves) would be enough for us, but Thérèse, like Jesus before her, wants happiness for the littlest, most imperfect souls as well as for the greatest and most perfect. Moreover, the point of the Little Way is that we don't have to wait to be holy (to grow up, to be perfect) to receive Jesus' love, and that wouldn't make sense anyhow, since it's His love that makes us holy.

What's really going on here is that Jesus wants to remain in us in the fullness of His Real Presence because that's the newest way He's proposing to satisfy the desires of our heart (as well as His). He is God. He made us. He knows the full range of our desires, and He's not asking us to give up most of them, but rather to share the entirety of them with Him, even as He shares the entirety of Himself with us. Let me be more specific.

In the case of the three friends with whom I first shared the news of this book and Jesus' outrageous idea, two were wives and mothers of many years, and the third was preparing for her wedding, a dream and desire of her heart that Jesus was fulfilling with all the love of His.

To take the last first, it was not surprising that a bride would be unprepared to sacrifice the attention due to her earthly bridegroom. But neither was it surprising, once I figured out what was going on, that my long married friends should be hesitant to respond to Jesus' wooing. The comical part is that no matter how long we've been following Him, no matter how many times we've heard about "states in life" and different vocations and their corresponding beauty, regardless of how familiar we are with the idea that we're all called to be Saints, finally, we imagine that the highest holiness is reserved for those who are in convents and monasteries. Because honestly, how can we focus entirely on Jesus in the midst of the "distractions" of our families, our work, our communities, and life in the world?

My friends love Jesus with all their hearts. They want to become Saints. They want to help their husbands and children become Saints, though they realize it's really Jesus' work and that if we can get dinner on the table, that's a good day for us and perhaps the most we can expect (or more!) from ourselves.

Still, they've wanted for years to please Jesus more than anything, and, I repeat, it's almost comical that now, when I've suggested a way to live in closer union with Him—closer than we had ever imagined we could be to Him, even without leaving the circle of our family within our homes—they are flabbergasted and flattened by what they think they must give Jesus in return for what He suggests giving to them. It's the darndest thing. Just when we least expected it, that most unexpected of virtues, humility, has crept in and makes my friends cover their faces with their hands, protecting their unworthy selves from Jesus' kisses.

The good news, which in this instance amounts to crucial information, is that Jesus is not asking us to abandon our husbands and children, our daily duties, our interests and distractions, our hobbies, our preoccupations, our work, our friendships, nor even our attempts to amuse ourselves and those we love, no matter how silly and futile those attempts may be, given the obvious choices provided by the entertainment industry.

I can appreciate my friends' hesitation. They have chosen—because they have been called to it—the vocation of marriage, and they are right to cling to this vocation. How bizarre it would be, how unnatural (and if it were a word, I would add: how un-supernatural), to accept Jesus' invitation to invite Him to remain in them if that means having to live as a nun in the midst of their families. How disastrous!

No wonder they've raised this objection: I can't ask Jesus to remain in me. I'm not ready to ask Him for the kind of recollection St. Anthony of Claret demanded of himself. I'm not even ready to give up dumb T.V. shows! It's one thing to commit to fifteen minutes of attempted prayer and recollection after Holy Communion at Mass, but I'm not ready to give up the rest of my life to continuous prayer and recollection. I feel terrible, but I'm not ready for this!

The answer to this objection is that Jesus is not asking this. He understands us perfectly. He made us, and more than that, He's attending to us every second of our lives so that He knows us through and through. The sparrow, worth half a penny in His day (or a quarter of a penny, if two were worth half), couldn't fall to the ground without His knowing and caring. How much more does He know and care for us! And He is all Love, so He would not selfishly ask something which would consign us to a lifetime of unhappiness, as if that could bring Him joy.

The reason He's called most of us to the Sacrament of Marriage is not simply to keep up the numbers. He delights in our delight, and since we are social animals, since we are made for companionship, not loneliness, He has given us marriage as a precursor to our complete union with Him in Heaven, as a sign and promise of that fuller union of the Beatific Vision, but also so that we may live in happiness on earth, even if it's often a Valley of Tears. He wants us to enjoy each other, to help each other, to attend to each other in our families, and in our communities.

Which means He's not going to give us a gift that requires us to abandon all that He's already given us and go commune with Him at church 24/7, nor even in a corner of the house (if we can find one and barricade everyone else out).

What Jesus is offering through St. Thérèse and her petition is nothing more nor less than remaining in us as in a tabernacle. Nothing less: that's what this book is about. But in a sense, nothing more, that's what I'm trying to say in answer to this objection. The prayer He wants us to make our own is not, "Remain in me as in a tabernacle, and never let me be distracted from You by the life You've already given me (which I now renounce)," but simply:

Remain in me as in a tabernacle, and never separate Yourself from me.

Jesus is the omnipotent one. It's His job to figure out how to never separate from us.

We are merely tiny infants when it comes to even such a seemingly small (or frighteningly large) thing as awareness of Who is holding us. It wouldn't make sense for a nursing mother to demand that her baby know what is happening while they are a nursing couple, and God doesn't demand that we understand what is happening when He remains in us as in a tabernacle. But just as the mother knows her baby needs what she gives, so Jesus knows we need what He is now offering to us. Not because of what we can do, but because of what He can do.

Objection 7: How is it possible that we, knowing our lack of recollection, could invite Jesus to remain in us Sacramentally without,

on our part, then living a lack of respect and reverence for the
Blessed Sacrament?

The only proper answer to this very proper objection is to quote the one who is pushing us to invite Jesus in, the only Saint I know of who came up with this on her own (instead of Jesus proposing it first). Funny thing, it wasn't the great St. Anthony Mary Claret who asked for this grace. He was the one, actually, who tried to blot it out of his diary and needed Our Lady and Jesus to reassure him that yes, no question, he was receiving this inestimable grace.

The truth is that the one who said, "I choose all!" is the one who was inspired to choose Jesus in the Blessed Sacrament to remain in her, and she, St. Thérèse by name, is asking us to do the same. So what would she say about our concern that to invite Jesus to remain in us, too, is bordering on (if not straight out) irreverence for Him in the Blessed Sacrament, since we know our shortcomings all too well.

I can only say that we know ourselves half as well as she knew herself, and Thérèse is giving us the green light, the thumbs up, the all clear. Yes, even to us! Because here is her own experience. She loved Jesus in the Blessed Sacrament with a reverence that we can only hope to approach. Not only that, she knew better than we how very bad she was at paying Him the attention that was His due.

Do you know this secret? Thérèse herself often fell asleep during her prescribed times of prayer before the Blessed Sacrament. While praying in the chapel she would fall asleep kneeling, and later wake to find her head on the floor once again. This understandably bothered her. After all, her primary vocation as a Carmelite was to pray. But then one day she was inspired to see this awkward situation through the eyes of Love. It occurred to her that parents delight in gazing upon their sleeping children, and so God, the ultimate Father, must delight in seeing His children asleep too. She reminds us as she reminded her sister Leonie, "God is even kinder than you think. He is satisfied with a look, a sigh of love."

Thérèse is not leading us astray, nor does she overestimate us. If she recommends that we invite Jesus to remain in us as in the tabernacle, it is because she knows that He is satisfied with a look, a sigh of love. And she knows, too, that He will not take it as a sign of disrespect, but a sign of great love, that we desire Him to live with us, Body, Blood, Soul, and Divinity, through everything we experience, even though we will be unable to attend to Him with more than our meager looks and sighs. That's okay. He will love to gaze on us, His children, no matter our inability to remember to gaze on Him. That we want Him with us is enough.

Objection 8: If we cultivate this desire and ask Jesus to grant it, how will we know if He has?

How will we know, that is, if Jesus in the Blessed Sacrament is remaining within us between our Communions?

Her confidence is so great that I believe Thérèse would rather we ask "How do we know *that* Jesus is remaining within us as in a tabernacle?" rather than "How do we know *if...*?" But either way, we must begin with how we *don't* know.

First, we must be clear that such knowledge (of Jesus' abiding Real Presence within us) cannot be had by the theological virtue of faith. This virtue of faith is how we know that Jesus' Real Presence abides in the Sacramental Species—on the altar after the consecration, in our Holy Communions until the species naturally corrupts within us, and reserved in our churches after the Holy Sacrifice of the Mass.

The Church teaches us that the Presence of Christ remains under the sacred species as long as the species of bread and wine remain—this was proclaimed formally and definitively at the

Council of Trent (Session XIII, *Decretum de ss. Eucharistia*, Canon 4: DS 1654). Such determinate doctrinal teachings, from the articles of the Creed to the dogmatic definition of the Assumption of Mary, are the proper objects of the virtue of faith.

Jesus has left us His visible Church so we will not wander aimlessly or confusedly after the truth. He who can neither deceive nor be deceived entrusts the Church with the solemn responsibility to guard the truths of revelation, and these truths are the proper objects of the faith our baptism has planted within us.

Private revelations—such as those in which Jesus informed St. Anthony Mary Claret, St. Faustina, and Blessed Dina of His abiding Eucharistic presence within them—are not the object of the divine gift of faith, but rather they are believed by an assent of human faith.

When Pope Benedict XVI was Cardinal Ratzinger and Prefect of the Congregation for the Doctrine of the Faith, he made this distinction (between public and private revelation, and the types of faith by which they are believed) in his theological commentary on the third part of the secret of Fatima. He wrote:

> 1. The authority of private revelations is essentially different from that of the definitive public Revelation. The latter demands faith, in it in fact God Himself speaks to us through human words and the mediation of the living community of the Church. Faith in God and in His word is different from any other human faith, trust, or opinion. The certainty that it is God who is speaking gives me the assurance that I am in touch with truth itself. It gives me a certitude that is beyond verification by any human way of knowing. It is the certitude upon which I build my life and to which I entrust myself in dying.
>
> 2. Private revelation is a help to this faith, and shows its credibility precisely by leading me back to the

definitive public Revelation. In this regard, Cardinal Prospero Lambertini, the future Pope Benedict XIV, says in his classic treatise, which later became normative for beatifications and canonizations: "An assent of Catholic faith is not due to revelations approved in this way; it is not even possible. These revelations seek rather an assent of human faith in keeping with the requirements of prudence, which puts them before us as probable and credible to piety."

Cardinal Ratzinger goes on to explain:

Ecclesiastical approval of a private revelation has three elements: the message contains nothing contrary to faith or morals; it is lawful to make it public; and the faithful are authorized to accept it with prudence. Such a message can be a genuine help in understanding the Gospel and living it better at a particular moment in time; therefore it should not be disregarded. It is a help which is offered, but which one is not obliged to use. (*The Last Secret of Fatima*, pp. 142-143)

These distinctions are imperative because we are all called to be Saints; we cannot be Saints without humility; and humility is truth. We are not getting to Heaven by making things up. There is no need, even, to re-invent the wheel.

We need to know that there is good reason to believe in the "something new" St. Thérèse has brought to our attention, has prayed for, has prayed that we will pray for; but our belief in this new thing, this Eucharistic miracle in which Jesus remains in the soul "as in a tabernacle," is not the same as our belief in the miracle that occurs at the consecration and when the Real Presence of Jesus remains in the consecrated Host in the tabernacle.

Our faith in Jesus' Real Presence in the Blessed Sacrament is faith in God and in His word, "faith" properly speaking. I would say our belief in this miracle of the conservation of the Sacred Species in a person between Communions is a combination of the theological virtue of faith (for it contains a belief in Jesus' Real Presence in the Blessed Sacrament), reason (we argue simply, with Thérèse, from God's omnipotence to His ability to do this), and human faith in the private revelations in the lives of the Saints who have experienced this "something new."

There is another way we will *not* know Jesus is fulfilling our request for His continuing sacramental presence within us. We have discussed at length that we will not know this miracle by faith, properly speaking. We can be equally sure that we will not know this miracle through our feelings. Even in the straightforward explanation Thérèse gave to Marie of the Trinity, although "this extraordinary feeling that you experience is proof that God lavishly grants all that you ask of Him," nonetheless, "usually His little 'victims of love' labor in faith; otherwise they could not live. The Real Presence will not make itself felt, but it is no less existential" (*Thérèse of Lisieux and Marie of the Trinity*, p. 70).

Thérèse knows that our feelings come and go, and furthermore that our feelings of consolation are not meant to be the standard of His love for us, so while her conviction that He will lavish His gifts upon us remains unshaken, she advises us not to look to our feelings for confirmation.

She has warned us that for simple souls there are no complicated ways, and we might blame this objection ("How do we know?") on our complexity, but I think that would be unfair. Thérèse surely wants us to know the truth, and the truth includes important distinctions made by theologians and Prefects of the Congregation for the Doctrine of the Faith to protect us from a false assurance or delusional mysticism.

How, then, shall we know? Thérèse provides the answer in her reply to Marie of the Trinity, and here it is:

> Is God not omnipotent? If we so desire, it would not be difficult for Him to make His sacramental presence in our souls remain from one Communion to the next ... One receives from God as much as one hopes for ... Yes, for His little 'victims of love,' He likes to make wondrous gifts which infinitely surpass their immense desires ... Nothing is impossible to the omnipotence of God and I am sure that He would not have inspired this request if He would not have wanted to realize it. (*Thérèse and Marie*, p. 70)

In her simplicity, however, St. Thérèse has an even shorter answer. "It is confidence, and nothing but confidence, that must lead us to Love." Thérèse counsels confidence, surrender, and gratitude. We can only follow her on the Little Way.

Objection 9: If we were given this grace of the abiding Real Presence of Jesus within us, wouldn't this make Holy Communion unnecessary, and dull our desire for receiving Him and spending time with Him "outside" of us?

This objection must be from the devil because it's so clever and insidious, but a quick look at the lives of the Saints and our own lives will tell another story.

If we were to examine the lives of those Saints who experienced this miracle—so far I am aware of Anthony Mary Claret, Faustina, Padre Pio, Margaret Mary, and Dina Belanger—we would see that the privilege of Jesus' "permanent residence" in them only increased their love and longing for Him.

To take one example, let's look at what St. Anthony Mary Claret wrote in his autobiography about his experiences after receiving this great grace. Far from lessening his devotion to the Holy Sacrifice of the Mass and the Blessed Sacrament reserved in church, the Real Presence of Christ within him only made him love Jesus outside of him even more. He writes:

> In the half hour immediately after Mass I am entirely consumed by God's grace and love. There is nothing I desire but to do His holy will. I live, but my life is that of Christ, and in possessing me, my poor Lord possesses a nothing, and I in possessing Him, possess everything. (*Autobiography*, p. 194)

St. Anthony is here relating his experiences of 1862, some months after Our Lord had told him (and confirmed on another occasion) that He had granted Anthony "the great grace of retaining the sacramental species."

Anthony goes on in the next chapter of his autobiography to describe how he felt at this time (again, after He was aware of the Blessed Sacrament residing always within him) when, daily, he made a visit to Jesus in church.

> When I am before the Blessed Sacrament, I feel so living a faith that I cannot possibly explain it. Jesus almost appears to me [another translation has here "Christ in the Eucharist is almost tangible to me"], and I continually kiss His wounds, and am finally embraced by Him. When the hour to leave strikes, I always have to use violence to wrench myself away from His divine presence. (p. 197)

We can see, then, that far from making St. Anthony indifferent to Jesus in the Blessed Sacrament outside him, this grace rather increased his longing to be with and remain with Jesus in the Holy Mass and in the Sacrament reserved in church.

But for simplicity's sake, as always our best and most obvious example is St. Thérèse. She is best because she is closest to us, "littlest," and the one who, like us (most of us, at least!), had no private revelation to confirm this miracle. She is most obvious because we can find in the voluminous literature about her the perfect incident to disprove our objection.

Let's start with her littleness. Despite it—that is despite her lack of explicit confirmation by God of this miracle—and yet because of it (she knew her littleness called down His mercy), Thérèse was confident God would lavishly grant all the petitions of her Act. As we just saw, she told Marie of the Trinity, "Nothing is impossible to the omnipotence of God and I am sure that He would not have inspired this request if He would not have wanted to realize it."

What exactly is this request? Thérèse prays in the Act: "I cannot receive Holy Communion as often as I desire, but, Lord, are You not all-powerful? Remain in me as in a tabernacle and never separate Yourself from Your little victim."

In replying to a previous objection, we mentioned a type of desire (our third category) that God initially does not seem to fulfill; later we see that He's found a more creative way to fulfillment than we had anticipated. Thérèse is always a step ahead of us—like a child, skipping and running and twirling about, she is almost ahead of her Father—and here she has identified a desire that God does not seem to answer: "I cannot receive Holy Communion as often as I desire." But then immediately she proposes a solution that will fully satisfy both parties: "Remain in me as in a tabernacle." Thérèse has thought up a creative way God can answer her desires even beyond what might have seemed likely.

What might have seemed likely? And why couldn't Thérèse receive Holy Communion as often as she desired?

Although daily Communion was not customary in the universal Church until after Thérèse's death when Pope Pius X allowed it (possibly due to Thérèse's intercession), nonetheless, during Thérèse's lifetime Pope Leo XIII had issued a decree recommending daily Communion for religious communities. Unfortunately, in the Lisieux Carmel, Pope Leo's decree was not brought into effect due to the timidity and scrupulosity of Mother Marie de Gonzague, the superior before and after Mother Agnes. How did this affect Thérèse?

We might think that, with her conviction that God had granted her all the requests of the Act, that is, with her confidence that the Blessed Sacrament remained within her, Thérèse wouldn't have minded that she couldn't receive Him daily in the consecrated Host. Wouldn't such reception be, after all, almost redundant since she already possessed and was possessed by Him? The answer is no. This was not at all the effect His Presence in her produced. Marie of the Sacred Heart tells us about her little sister:

> At Carmel, her great suffering had been not being able to receive Communion each day. She said, a short time before her death, to Mother Marie de Gonzague, who was afraid of daily Communion:
>
> "Mother, when I'm in Heaven, I'll make you change your opinion."
>
> This is what happened. After the death of the Servant of God, the chaplain gave us Communion every day, and Mother Marie de Gonzague, instead of being repelled by it, was very happy about it. (*Last Conversations*, p. 262)

Before her death, however, Thérèse knew it was impossible to attain this miracle of daily Communion, so she worked around it with her prayer tucked into the Act of Oblation. And yet her conviction that He had granted this request (of remaining in her as in a tabernacle) did not lessen her desire to receive Him in Holy Communion, nor her suffering when she was deprived of Him there.

The Holy Eucharist is called the Mystery of Faith, and here is another mystery tied up with it: Thérèse possesses Jesus (or better, He possesses her) continuously, though without feeling

His Presence, by a Eucharistic miracle. Yet she desires Him no less in the sensible reception of Holy Communion, where He will be truly "sensed" but only through the accidental forms of the bread and wine.

I didn't realize how much Thérèse continued to desire Him in Holy Communion until I came across an episode of her life I had never heard or read before. Again, it is from *Last Conversations.* This incident is recorded by Mother Agnes and dated August 20, 1897, forty days before Thérèse's death.

> With reference to Communion which she felt she could no longer receive in the future, and as a consequence of many reflections she had heard on the subject, this day was one of intense agony for her and of temptations, too, which I imagine were terrible. She begged me in the afternoon to keep silent and not even to look at her. She whispered: "I would cry too much if I were to tell you my troubles right now, and I'm having such difficulty in breathing that I would certainly suffocate." She spoke to me after a silence of at least an hour, but she was so much disturbed that she held before her eyes the fan she had been given to chase away the flies.

What was it about Communion that had so disturbed Thérèse? A footnote reveals, from another notebook of Mother Agnes, the following details:

> She had terrible agonies to suffer that day. This is the reason for them: Holy Communion, so much desired by her, became a source of torment during her illness. Because of her vomiting, her breathing difficulties, her weakness, she feared accidents and she would have preferred that we tell her not to receive. She did not want to take this responsibility upon herself, but since

she had said nothing, we believed she was in agreement with us when we insisted that she receive Communion. She continued to be silent, but that day she was unable to restrain herself any longer, and she fell into tears. We didn't know to what we should attribute her sadness, and we begged her to tell us. However, the choking produced by her sobs was so violent that, not only was she unable to answer us, but she made a sign to us not to say a word, not even to look at her. At the end of several hours, having remained alone with her, I dared to approach her and tell her that I had guessed the source of her tears. I consoled her as well as I could, and she seemed close to dying of sorrow. Never had I seen her in such agony. She did not receive Communion from then on right up to her death. (p. 157)

As I wrote this chapter and tried to find the foregoing passage, as if that weren't enough in itself, I came across this further illustration of Thérèse's love for Jesus in Holy Communion. Mother Agnes writes of an earlier incident, from May of 1897:

One day, when she attended Mass and received Communion, although shortly before she had received a vesicatory (blistering), I began to cry and was unable to attend the Divine Office. I followed her into her cell, and I shall always see her seated on her little bench, her back supported by a partition of rough boards. She was quite exhausted and was gazing at me with a sad but very gentle look! My tears redoubled, and, guessing how much I was causing her to suffer, I begged pardon on my knees. She said simply: "This is not suffering too much to gain one Communion!" To repeat the phrase is nothing; one had to hear her state it. (*Last Conversations*, p. 255)

The Saints tell us that if we saw Jesus we would die of love, unless He sustained us ... I think that if we only saw the love of the Saints for Him, that would be enough to stop the beating of our poor unloving hearts!

Seeing Thérèse's great desire for Holy Communion, we may be tempted to think our own desire much too weak to attain to her heights. But remember, we are not seeking to climb the mountain of love—with Thérèse, we must become smaller and smaller and depend entirely on Jesus to be our elevator to the summit of sanctity.

Meanwhile, what of our attempts to imitate her in praying the Act, in offering ourselves to Merciful Love, in asking for this Eucharistic miracle?

Here is what I've found for myself.

I don't know how to pray well. Often when I try to recite or read prayers my mind wanders away from the words—sometimes even before I've started. But wanting to pray this Act of Oblation, wanting to mean it, I've had some success in taking it phrase by phrase. And when I get to the part about "Remain in me"? Well, to get to that place, I must first cross the bridge of "I cannot receive Holy Communion as often as I desire." Knowing that I have to mean what I say for these words to bring me closer to God, I try to mean them.

And here's where we come to the Choose Your Own Adventure portion of this book.

If you are a theologian or extremely devout (and these need not be mutually exclusive!), I recommend you choose (a), immediately following this paragraph. If you are the rest of us, choose (b), below.

(a) "I cannot receive Holy Communion as often as I desire." This means I need to desire Holy Communion: Often, or how else could it be true that I can't receive Him in the consecrated Host as often as I desire?

But if I desire Him very much, then I will *try* to receive Him —a real desire does not stop at the feeling. One sign of the authenticity of our desires (their worthiness of the name, and thus our confidence that they are inspired by God and therefore He will fulfill them) is our willingness to pursue their attainment.

And so, the next thing I know, saying this prayer I am re-evaluating my day. Can I receive Holy Communion today? Is there any possibility? What can I adjust in my schedule? Because surely I can't honestly say that I can't receive Holy Communion as often as I desire if I don't desire it much and if I don't work to make that desire come true as much as is in my power.

I have known many, many people who inspire me by their faithfulness to daily Communion. A favorite example is that of Dr. Ron McArthur, who would say as his highest form of praise, "He's a daily communicant!" There was a kind of awe in his voice when he said this about someone, so that it was years before I realized that he, Dr. McArthur, was also a daily communicant! He was a humble man, so I don't think he thought of himself this way, but he always admired those he saw making efforts and sacrifices to get closer to receiving Jesus as often as they desired.

Which brings me to my next observation. The more we love, the more we want to be with the Beloved. As we fall more and more in love with Jesus, is it possible that daily Communion (even if our circumstances permit it) will be enough union with Him? I don't think so. I think that as we love Him more, as we realize His Real Presence, Body, Blood, Soul and Divinity in the Blessed Sacrament, spending fifteen minutes daily possessing Him and being possessed by Him in this closest-of-unions available to us on earth can't possibly be enough.

❧❀

(b) "I cannot receive Holy Communion as often as I desire." This means I need to desire Holy Communion: Often, or how else could it be true that I can't receive Him in the consecrated Host as often as I desire?

One might think the next step, then, would be to desire more than anything to go to daily Mass in order to receive daily Holy Communion. Or, given the new Code of Canon Law, one's desire could even climb to the level of desiring to attend Mass twice a day in order to receive Jesus twice a day in Communion, which is now allowed.

If you find every adventure irresistible (or feel like you might miss something if you skip a few paragraphs), you may have read in (a) above that my initial reaction to seriously praying the Act and desiring this grace was to then desire daily Mass and Communion. That is true.

But this would not be a complete book nor a convincing one (for the little ones) if I didn't include the sequel to that first reaction.

Although I was raised Catholic, my first exposure to daily Mass and Communion was in college. That was where I fell in love with Jesus and couldn't get enough of Him. Mass was offered three times a day on the small campus where I lived, studied, and spent almost all my time. It was the easiest thing in the world to go daily—early, if I was up early; mid-day, if I didn't go in the morning (and classes and lunch were scheduled to allow everyone to attend the mid-day Mass, as well as the other two Masses, come to think of it); or before dinner if that was the best option. It was awesome.

And this practice of daily Mass and Communion meant so much to me that I asked the priest who married us (one, holy, Catholic Father Gerard Steckler, S.J.) to please mention in his homily something about our devout hope that daily Mass and Communion would be the status quo for my husband and me throughout our marriage. He was an extremely obliging fellow, and he not only mentioned it, he waxed eloquent.

Devout hopes are so very good. I don't want to discourage any such delightful aspirations in you, dear reader, but I must tell you the sequel, both to the homily and to my praying the Act.

There have been times in my married life when daily Mass and Communion were possible. And then there have been times, many, many more times when I have found daily Mass and Communion impossible.

I know people (some are dear friends), married and with more children and more obligations than I have, for whom daily Mass and Communion are non-negotiable. This practice is possible because they make it possible, because they see its importance and they prioritize and it happens. I admire them tremendously and consider this habit a very special and inestimable grace in their lives.

I have not been given this grace, and though I've frequently requested it, I remember what many wise, experienced and holy priests (including the one who married us) have told me, and which I believe with all my heart. Daily Mass and Communion, although an excellent thing (perhaps the best thing!) are not an obligation. This much we know from our catechism and the constant teaching of the Church. But furthermore, it might be the case that God, in calling us to the duties of our married state in life, might be calling us (for a time) to sacrifice the daily Sacrifice of the Mass and Holy Communion.

And like the grace of His remaining in me as in a tabernacle, this grace, too, of His coming to me daily at Mass and in Holy Communion is something only He can accomplish.

So that after my initial reaction to this wondrous petition of the Act, which reaction was, once again, to try and force His hand by trying to force daily Mass and Communion to be the ordinary and perennial course of my life in exile, I had to admit defeat. Again.

Which is when I began to realize Jesus' extraordinary (divine, really) delicacy and solicitude in His infinite love for me. Knowing that we couldn't meet daily at church, He found a way for us to not only meet but to remain constantly united even as I stayed at home.

Not that I'm saying I "know" Jesus has answered my prayer that He remain in me as in a kind of perpetual Holy Communion. But rather, I see that He has given me a new desire (for this perpetual union) which brings with it peace regarding my state in life. As a wife and mother, as a person with obligations in the world, rather than in the cloister, I can hope to live with Jesus' Real Presence in me, even when it would be "crazy making" or the equivalent of twisting myself into a spiritual pretzel to try and insist on receiving Him every day at Mass.

With those who, by God's grace, do make it to daily Mass in the midst of their family obligations, I rejoice in their (and His) daily Communions. And I offer this book's "something new" as a way to prolong those Communions so that He does not leave them between one Mass and the next.

But for those little ones who find, as I do, daily Mass beyond their capacities, I offer this Eucharistic grace as a remedy. Jesus will be delighted to remain in you as in a tabernacle between Sunday Communions, and you need not fear that your littleness distresses Him. After all, our desires are not the last word. He is.

As Thérèse responded to her sister Marie of the Sacred Heart, our patroness in the little way of objections and hesitations:

> How can you say that my desires are the sign of my love? Ah! I really feel that it is not this at all that pleases God in my little soul; what pleases Him is that He sees me loving my littleness and my poverty, the blind hope I have

in His mercy. This is my only treasure; why should this treasure not be yours?

❧✱

While Thérèse points out that her desires are not her true wealth, she does not deny that her desires are nearly endless. She originally wrote "infinite" to describe them to Jesus in her Act, and though she changed that word to "immense" to please the theologian who gave an unofficial imprimatur to her prayer, she always regretted that he had asked for that change.

We haven't heard the last from our objections. We've mentioned and answered some first ones here, but this is too great a grace to simply float down like a rose petal from Heaven. And yet I'm sure that in her mission to make us love God as she loves Him, among her remaining desires Thérèse cherishes this one: that we will ask Jesus for this Eucharistic miracle.

Our confidence may waver, but hers is now confirmed and validated by the fullness of knowledge only possible through the Beatific Vision. If on earth she so wanted this miracle for her sisters and a whole legion of little souls she had not yet met, in Heaven she can only be more adamant in her insistence that we adhere to the Truth, and let Him adhere to us.

Jesus is waiting patiently, waiting for us to surrender and let Him remain in us. Don't worry if you still don't feel ready. His patience, too, is divine. And then Thérèse knows our littleness and won't leave us to work this out alone. She has plenty of roses left to distribute, and much more to say to convince us that truly, it is our littleness that He loves.

Part III

More Reasons to Believe

Chapter 6

Thérèse's Solution

*O Jesus! Why can't I tell all little souls how
unspeakable is Your condescension? I feel that if
You found a soul weaker and littler than mine, You
would be pleased to grant it still greater favors.*

—St. Thérèse, *Story of a Soul*

You might wonder why we need another solution. After all, is there still a problem?

We've seen that God likes Thérèse's petition—He had granted it to St. Anthony Mary Claret thirty-three years before Thérèse composed the Act, and He granted it to other Saints after her time.

We've seen that Thérèse did indeed intend all little souls to ask for this outrageous grace, and that one of those she assisted in asking, sensibly felt the petition answered—though Thérèse's novice, Marie of the Trinity, didn't dare explain what this feeling of the Eucharistic Jesus in her meant. Thérèse, however, did dare explain it and told Marie, "Yes! He is granting this grace! He wants to lavish these graces on all little souls."

So what's the problem?

Call it a crisis of confidence, but while I love praying the Act of Oblation, I continue (even after answering nine objections) to have a hard time believing that this grace is meant for me. I didn't need my husband's reality check to see I'm no St. Anthony Mary Claret, no St. Faustina, no St. Padre Pio, no St. Margaret Mary, no Blessed Dina. And while I absolutely believe Thérèse about everything—therefore even what she says about her own littleness—I'm no St. Thérèse either.

The Maries help a lot: Marie of the Sacred Heart with her aversion for suffering; Marie of the Trinity with her awareness of radical unworthiness. These I can relate to, and they were assured by Thérèse that this Offering was for them too. And Céline? I like that she didn't even get a say in the matter. We don't know what objections she would have raised. Thérèse didn't give her a chance!

But now, when it comes to us, what will Thérèse say to our hesitations?

She has a blanket answer to every objection we can dream up—and by myself, I can dream up plenty—so let's start there. All her answers come back to the same fundamental principles, the same solution, and her style reminds me of St. Thomas in the *Summa* occasionally saving time answering objections by saying simply, "From what has been said, the objections are easily solved."

Similarly, we can deduce St. Thérèse's solution from the answers we've gathered already.

She said to Marie of the Trinity, "It's your knowledge of your unworthiness that makes you ready." To her sister Marie of the Sacred Heart, she said, "What pleases Him is that He sees me loving my littleness and my poverty, the blind hope that I have in His mercy. That is my only treasure: why would this treasure not be yours?" And again to her sister Marie, "To love Jesus, to be His victim of Love, the weaker one is, without desires or virtues, the more suited one is for the workings of this consuming and transforming Love. The desire alone to be a victim suffices, but we must consent to remain always poor and without strength, and that is the difficulty" (*Letters*, pp. 999-1000; Letter 197).

This is funny. We think that the difficulty—the real obstacle to our receiving the graces of the great Saints—is that we are always poor and without strength. St. Thérèse says, *au contraire*, the difficulty is precisely our refusing to *remain* poor and without strength!

This word "remain" reminds us of our problem. Thérèse wants us to ask Jesus to remain in us in a very concrete way—none of this vague, "God is everywhere; the risen Christ expands to fill the universe" kind of presence for her. She wants His Real Sacramental Eucharistic Body-Blood-Soul-and-Divinity Presence to stay within her, and within us, so that finally we can begin with her to satiate Jesus' tremendous thirst for our love.

How many scenes in the Gospel reveal the gentle, tender love of His Sacred Heart and His longing to be with the children of men? We would have to say all of them. It would be a wonderful exercise to count the scenes in the four Gospels: from some, His mercy would shine out almost blindingly. In others, we might have to look more closely, but surely His kindness and longing are at the bottom of everything. We are talking about the One who said of Himself, "Learn from Me, for I am gentle and humble of heart."

He is the same yesterday, today, and forever. He still thirsts, as He did at the well when He asked the Samaritan woman for a drink, as He did on the cross when He cried out. He could barely speak, had to raise Himself by pushing His torn and bloody feet against the nails that held Him fast to the cross, but he did it in order to call to us, "I thirst!" And yet neither on the cross nor at the well did He accept a drink. He was thirsting for our love, and as Thérèse makes clear, He still thirsts.

"Ah!" she writes:

> I feel it more than ever before, Jesus is parched, for He meets only the ungrateful and indifferent among His disciples in the world, and among His own disciples, alas, He finds few hearts who surrender to Him without reservations, who understand the real tenderness of His infinite Love. How fortunate we are to understand the intimate secrets of our Spouse. (*Story of a Soul*, p. 189)

Thérèse expressed all kinds of desires in her short life. She was constantly amazed at how God fulfilled these desires, and this in turn filled her with confidence, which then fueled her desires all the more—like a bonfire, the flames burning brighter and hotter until the blaze reached high into the Heavens.

She frequently gives us examples of how God fulfilled her desires, and how she responded. From her sickbed she told Mother Agnes:

> I had made a complete sacrifice of Sister Geneviéve (Céline), but I can't say that I no longer desired her here. Very often in the summer, during the hour of silence before Matins, while I was seated on the terrace, I would say to myself: Ah! If only my Céline were near me! No! This would be too great a happiness for this earth.
>
> And this seemed to me an unrealizable dream. However, it wasn't through selfishness that I desired this happiness; it was for her soul, it was so that she walk our way ... And when I saw her enter here, and not only enter, but was given to me completely to be instructed in all things, when I saw that God was doing

this, thus surpassing all my desires, I understood what an immensity of love He has for me.

And so, little Mother, if a desire that is hardly expressed is answered in such a way, it is then impossible that all my great desires about which I've so frequently spoken to God will not be completely answered. (*Last Conversations*, pp. 100-101)

I must say I know how Thérèse feels, for I once had an unspoken, unselfish desire of mine answered beyond my wildest dreams. A dear friend had died. She was one who repeated after Thérèse, "The Little Way only," and she was very evidently purified by Love before her death. I wanted to tell everyone who knew her that they needn't doubt her soul's quick flight to Heaven. Hadn't St. Thérèse said, "For those who love, there is no purgatory"? And my friend had definitely loved.

I'd written her a letter before she died, telling her about this aspect of Thérèse's doctrine and how Jesus was waiting for her soul to fly to Him. He had purified her already, and it was time for her to bypass purgatory and dart into His eternal embrace. Without my having asked or even imagined such a possibility, after the funeral, to a packed church of those who knew her, my letter was read from the pulpit.

So I know what Thérèse means about God's ability to answer even our unspoken prayers, and how that softens our hard hearts. But I'm still far behind her in gratitude, and I'm also staggered by her example of how much confidence is possible. I would have thought that well before this episode with Céline's entrance, Thérèse had plenty of confidence, a fullness even. But no, with each additional sign of God's love, with each additional answer to her prayers (spoken and unspoken), she is more and more sure that He will fulfill her other desires as well.

What were some of these other desires?

If we start with those we know He has answered, we can take note that she died a martyr (a martyr of love); she became a missionary—both through the missionary activity of her adopted spiritual brothers and through the Church's naming her patroness of the missions; she has been allowed to spend her Heaven doing good on earth: through the dissemination of her writings, through the Church's approbation of her Little Way, and through her shower of roses.

One of my favorite stories about St. Thérèse comes from a certain Monseigneur de Teil. In 1896, he gave a talk in the parlour of the Lisieux Carmel and Thérèse was among the assembled nuns who heard him. Father de Teil was then postulator for the cause of the Carmelite martyrs of Compiegne, who had offered themselves for France and were guillotined at the end of the French Revolution. When Father finished his talk, he said to Thérèse and her religious sisters, "Listen! If any of you ever plan on being canonized, please, have mercy on your poor postulator: work a lot of miracles!" Several years later de Teil found himself the vice-postulator of Thérèse's cause and said, "She is a very obedient child!" because she did provide for him, as he'd ordered her when she was alive, plenty of miracles!

Despite the evidence that God surely answers Thérèse's desires, our problem is in believing her that we, too, can fruitfully make this petition to God. Why don't we, then, approach this from another direction.

Her solution is, first, to remind us that God chooses the weak, and the weaker we are, the more impoverished, the more perfectly we are suited for His action, for the designs of His love within us. So far so good; we fit the description.

Second, she was confident that since she had never denied God anything, He would not deny her anything. We have vast proof that He has not denied her any number of things. This last little thing, His Presence remaining sacramentally in us as in the tabernacle, we then have reason to believe He will grant as well—at her request, for He does not deny her anything. Since she is asking this for us too, even if we are not confident He will grant our own petition for this grace—speaking for myself I'm sorry to say I have denied Him many things—still we have good reason to think He'll grant this favor to us for her sake.

But ultimately, He loves us too. And if there is an argument to convince us that God will answer our petitions, St. Thérèse has provided it in the very words of her prayer.

She begins with Jesus' own indisputable words, "If you ask anything of the Father in My name, He will give it to you." She moves on to the truth she first learned from St. John of the Cross and has confirmed through her own experience: "The more You want to give, the more You make us desire." She announces a fervent desire that appears to be unanswered: "I cannot receive Holy Communion as often as I desire." And then, she offers God the solution, along with her full confidence, "But Lord, are you not all-powerful? Remain in me as in a tabernacle."

Finally, her most compelling argument is, once again, who we are and who God is. When my husband and I first entered Carmel as secular members of the Order, a wise Carmelite priest told us that a good starting place for prayer, one recommended by St. Teresa of Avila, was to consider, to ask (since prayer is a conversation with the One whom we know loves us), "Who are You, God, and who am I?"

Thérèse knew. She knew God was all-powerful Love, and she was His little creature who depended upon Him for everything. So in this too, she depended upon Him. She did not think she deserved for Him to remain in her as in a tabernacle, but she knew His delight was to be with the children of men, that He longed (because He is so good, for our sakes, but in His great mystery, because He is love, somehow for Himself too) to stay with us ... So she simply asked Him, and reminded Him of a few important reasons why He should listen to her. First, He promised He would. And second, this was nothing difficult for Him to achieve: easy-peasy on His side, you might say, not to speak irreverently, but to acknowledge how almighty He is.

When the Church looks at a person to judge whether he or she exhibited heroic virtue (which is not the virtue of a super-hero, but God's virtue infused in the human soul and thus evidence of that soul's union with Him), the first virtues examined are faith, hope, and charity.

St. Thérèse said she was very little, and since she always spoke the truth, we should believe her. But she was also great, not in herself but because she believed so thoroughly what God had revealed about Himself. He has revealed that He is all-powerful Love, and because she believed Him, believed in Love, she hoped that He would (of course, it follows from who He is) take perfect care of her and grant all her desires. Because He was so good, she loved Him—but not having much ability on her own, she asked Jesus to accept her childlike love and then stay in her so He could more properly love His Father and her neighbors through her, from within her, and thus, she could fulfill His commandments.

I love St. Thérèse so much, for reasons too many to catalogue here, but one of them is because she is, as she had wanted to be, imitable. With her sister Marie of the Sacred Heart, I can't say I desire suffering (I've often said that if I were God, I would get rid of suffering and free will), nor do I desire everything Thérèse desired. But if we are to believe her that it is her very littleness that makes her pleasing to God, and her blind hope in His mercy, these are things I can strive to imitate. I can try to believe that He is loving, hope that He will care for me, love Him to the best of my little powers, and yes, even ask Him in the most Blessed

Sacrament to remain in me as in a tabernacle, so that He can love His Father and our brothers through me.

I hope you are willing to join me in taking this leap. I'm not sure I know what I'm doing, but Thérèse does. And so, we had better move along with her to see what Love will show us next.

Chapter 7

Trying to Understand the Love
of the Heart of God

*God is even kinder than you think. He is
satisfied with a look, a sigh of love.*

—St. Thérèse, to Léonie, 1896

When I find myself thinking, despite Thérèse's words of en-couragement, that this time we have surely gone off the deep end—and I do find myself thinking this fairly frequently these days—there is an argument that never fails to make me think again, and more peacefully, like the child at rest in his father's arms, the child that Thérèse, and God before her, would have us imitate.

I don't even know if my "argument" deserves the name, for it is simply this:

Love never leaves anything undone.

Now if you're going to follow me on this one, I should say straight off that I don't mean *my* love never leaves anything undone. I'm afraid many things are left undone this very minute, if we're talking about my love. But I'm talking about Real Love, Plato's

Form of Love, Love in its purest, most perfect instantiation—ultimately, not that He's an instantiation, but ultimately: God.

God is love, St. John tells us. And Love (that is God, then) never leaves anything undone. St. John didn't say that second thing (to my knowledge), but I say it, because it's true. And I know it because that's the image we all share of true love, that's why we say silly things like "I'd cross the seven seas for love," and when we think about a saying like that, we believe it is actually, in the end, true. That is, if someone loved, no obstacle would be too great for that person to try, at least, to overcome. And if that Person had unlimited power, then surely no obstacle would be too great, and thus that Person would leave nothing undone in His quest for union with the beloved.

The big secret of the Saints—every one of them, each and all—is that they glimpsed God's love, and they were never the same again.

I love the passage in the First Book of Samuel where the boy Samuel, sleeping in the temple, keeps waking up the old priest Eli because he thinks Eli is calling him. The Scripture clearly states that God is calling Samuel, Samuel repeatedly goes to Eli, and Eli keeps telling the boy, "I did not call you, my son. Go back to sleep. " And here is my favorite part: "At that time Samuel was not familiar with the Lord, because the Lord had not revealed anything to him as yet" (1 Samuel 3: 1-10). This despite the fact that Samuel had lived with the Lord in the temple for many years already.

The initiative, as always, is with God. But if you are reading this book, my guess is that you are familiar with the Lord, that He has taken the initiative already, that you too have had at least a glimpse of His love.

And wouldn't you say, even after a mere glimpse, that His is the kind of love, or rather, He is that Love, which leaves nothing undone?

Imagine a parent with a sick child. Okay, not you or me with a sick child—in my case, because God has given me little to complain about, I find myself, late at night, trying to convince my child he's not really sick; I'm so tired and want to go to bed, and he doesn't seem very sick (let's say he's fighting a mild cold). But imagine instead the mom in one of those movies where the child is seriously ill and the doctor can't figure out what's wrong. There is the heroic mother, researching, investigating every possibility, questioning every medical professional. That mother, because of her love, will stop at nothing until she finds a diagnosis, and then a cure. This is love leaving nothing undone, and it rings true.

To take an example from the Gospels, think of the friends of the paralytic. They loved him, so they wanted to bring him into contact with Jesus who could heal him. There was no reasonable way to get their friend to the Divine Physician: Jesus was in a house crowded beyond its capacity. What could they do?

Since there was no reasonable way, the friends were forced to come up with an unreasonable way, a preposterous way, for love leaves nothing undone. Can't you picture them? Love overcomes all obstacles, so they climbed on top of the house, found a way to pull their paralyzed friend up there with them, cut a hole in the roof, and lowered him down into Jesus' lap! This is love, and He was not shocked, but so pleased that He immediately forgave the man's sins and healed his paralysis, without even being asked.

Which just goes to show that God too, God especially, will leave nothing undone. He has left nothing undone—after becoming one of us, He lived a life of poverty which culminated in His being mocked, scourged, crowned with thorns, and crucified, not to mention spit upon, derided, calumniated, slapped, and made to carry a heavy cross on His bruised muscles and torn skin. After His resurrection His body, glorified, could suffer no more—except that He had found a way, because love leaves nothing undone, to stay with us even after His Ascension into Heaven.

He chose to stay hidden under the appearances of bread and wine, which means that He remains subject to us. As Father Jean D'Elbée says in *I Believe in Love*, "The priest puts the Host on the left, it remains on the left. He places it on the right, it remains on the right! Those who profane it come, they take Him from His tabernacle and throw Him into the gutter; He lets Himself be thrown into the gutter" (pp. 250-251).

Now let's ask why. Why did God, having saved us, devise this most humble way to stay with us?

St. Thérèse explained, "It is not to remain in a golden ciborium that He comes to us each day from Heaven; it's to find another Heaven, infinitely more dear to Him than the first: the Heaven of our soul, made to His image, the living temple of the adorable Trinity" (*Story of a Soul*, p. 104). And I'm certain she would go on to explain, "Nor is it to remain in the Heaven of our souls for only fifteen minutes."

Remember: love leaves nothing undone.

Which is why it makes sense to me that God, Love, should leave nothing undone in this matter of His union with us in the Blessed Sacrament.

I had the privilege of editing a selection of sermons by a former teacher, a great Jesuit who was a disciple of St. Thomas Aquinas (and shared his name, for my teacher was Father Thomas Aquinas McGovern). The first sermon in the book is for the first Sunday of Advent, and Father McGovern follows St. Thomas in asking "Whether it was right, fitting—*utrum fuerit conveniens*—that God become man." Relaying St. Thomas' answer, Father McGovern tells us:

> Anything will be suitable to God and fitting to Him which in like manner can be said to flow from His

essence. But the very essence of God as infinite perfection is goodness. Whatever therefore is proper to goodness as such will be the kind of thing that will belong naturally to God from His very essence. But our experience attests to it that if goodness as such has any proper characteristic, it is that it is *sui diffusivum*: it tends to burst from its confines, to spread out, to share and communicate itself. Our desires to share our joys, the tendency of life to communicate life, are cases in point … It is this tendency on the part of Divine goodness to share and communicate itself that accounts for creation in the first place.

But if it is consonant with the Divine nature, as good, so to communicate goodness by creation, it is even more consonant with that same Divine nature, as the greatest good, to communicate that Divine goodness in the greatest possible way. And there is a way possible for God to communicate goodness to man, greater even than by creation, and this is so to unite a human nature with Himself as to make with the infinite God one person. Such a communication as this is perfectly in harmony with the Divine goodness—just the kind of thing, in other words, that God as infinite goodness might be expected to do. (*Selected Sermons of Thomas Aquinas McGovern, S.J.*, pp. 3-4)

I love this so much! Who, but a brilliant Saint, would suggest that (in Father McGovern's charming, colloquial style) the Incarnation is "just the kind of thing, in other words, that God as infinite goodness might be expected to do"? And who but St. Thomas would come up with unassailable reasoning to argue that the Incarnation is not merely fitting, but the kind of thing we can expect from God, who is so good?

Along these lines, it occurs to me that the Blessed Sacrament, too, once the infinitely creative, infinitely solicitous love of God had devised it, is another thing we perhaps could have expected, given His infinite goodness … And then, well, given that God's generous and resourceful love has ensured His abiding Presence among us, and given Thérèse's truth that it is not to stay in the ciborium or tabernacle that He is here … It seems to me almost inevitable that, since it is the nature of love to leave nothing undone, He should eventually choose to reside with us for a longer period of time by means of the conservation of the Most Blessed Sacrament within us.

When I discovered that St. Anthony Mary Claret experienced this great grace before Thérèse did, I began to read what I could find about his Eucharistic miracle, and in his biography I read that he was not the first person to experience this miracle. According to Venerable Mary of Agreda's *Mystical City of God*, the Blessed Virgin Mary was the first to receive this grace, retaining her Son's Real Presence within her between her Communions.

In the past, I had only heard of Venerable Mary of Agreda as the Spanish nun who wrote the life of the Blessed Virgin. Digging deeper, I found she was also—documentably, historically, without question—the Saint who bilocated more than 500 times from 1620 to 1631 to the American Southwest (New Mexico and Texas) in order to catechize and convert the Native Americans there.

Our modern skeptical era is so careful to protect us from the awesome power and mercy of God that I had never heard anything about Venerable Mary's wonderful mission to America. Interestingly, God had first shown her the places in the world where people lived in darkness and were least disposed to seek Him. Venerable Mary then begged Him for these peoples' conversion, and God sent her to do the converting. God gave her a desire and then miraculously fulfilled it, His love, once again, stopping at nothing. But it gets better.

Regarding the *Mystical City of God*, Venerable Mary's biographer James Carrico tells us in *The Life of Venerable Mary of Agreda* that the Blessed Mother spent ten years trying to get this universally revered Mother Superior to record her (the Blessed Mother's) autobiography. Finally Venerable Mary gave in, spent years taking dictation from Our Lady, and then was relieved to be done. Philip II had a copy made for himself. When a visiting confessor told Venerable Mary to burn the manuscript, she agreeably did so. I am in awe of her detachment! Her regular confessor returned, was peeved, and insisted she write the book again. The Blessed Mother was on his side, and Venerable Mary spent several more years re-writing. When she was done and handed over the new book, it was found to agree almost exactly with the copy belonging to Philip II.

I tell you all this because I have no idea what to make of *The Mystical City of God*. Impressive people like St. Anthony Mary Claret, and more recently the humble Capuchin Blessed Solanus Casey, cherished the book and read it frequently, deriving great profit from it. On the other hand, I suspect that our heroine, St. Thérèse, would not have been so fond of it, since she said:

> How I would have loved to be a priest in order to preach about the Blessed Virgin! One sermon would be sufficient to say everything I think about this subject. I'd first make people understand how little is known by us about her life ... For a sermon on the Blessed Virgin to please me and do me any good, I must see her real life, not her imagined life. I'm sure that her real life was very simple ... they should present her as imitable, bringing out her virtues, saying that she lived by faith just like ourselves, giving proofs of this from the Gospel. (*Last Conversations*, p. 161)

I have derived the most profit from reading St. Thérèse (after the Gospels), so I leave to one side the question of what to do

with the *Mystical City of God*, but I will say that given Venerable
Mary of Agreda's wondrous life, I don't think we can dismiss her
book. And if Thérèse had known of it, I'm sure she would have
been thrilled with what is said there about Our Lady's reception
of the grace that is the subject of *this* book.

Venerable Mary presents a moving argument that since Christ
promised at His Ascension to remain with His disciples always,
until the end of time, but they didn't in those early days have
the luxury of tabernacles and physical churches, it made perfect
sense that, though they didn't necessarily discern His Presence
in her precisely in this way, Our Lord had fulfilled His promise
by remaining in Our Lady as in a tabernacle.

This understanding of Our Lady's great grace would please
Thérèse because it fits Our Lady's simplicity. According to Venerable
Mary, the Blessed Virgin is the first to experience this continuous
Real Presence of Our Lord, but she experiences it in a hidden way.

Mary of Agreda says much about this miracle in Our Lady,
even offering an explanation of the mode by which the Blessed
Sacrament physically remained in her between Communions.
St. Thérèse never said anything about how precisely Jesus was to
fulfill this miracle in little souls, but the main point I appreciate
on her behalf (and ours) is that, according to Venerable Mary,
Jesus had fulfilled this miracle in His Blessed Mother.

Another account of this miracle in Mary comes from the
Flemish Benedictine wonderworker, Fr. Paul of Moll, who died
in 1896. He was a friend to the poor, healer of many who came
seeking cures, and counselor and confidant to people of rank not
only in his native Belgium, but also in England, France, Austria,
and Italy. His biographer, Edward van Speybrouck, reports that
Fr. Paul told a friend in the confessional:

> From the time of the Ascension of our Lord, the most
> Blessed Virgin communicated every day and by a special

privilege, the host remained intact within her up to the moment of the next Communion, so that Mary always guarded, in her interior, the humanity and divinity of Jesus Christ; and thus was able to keep up a continual conversation with her Divine Son. (*Father Paul of Moll*, p. 238)

We have reason to believe, then, that the goodness of God long ago decided to extend His continuing Eucharistic Presence beyond the tabernacle and into one very beloved soul. But aside from this unique case of Our Lady, it seems that Our Lord has waited until closer to our own times to manifest this miracle.

With the exceptions of St. Margaret Mary, who died in 1690, and the holy mystic Jeanne Benigne Gojos (another Visitation nun, who received her habit from St. Jane Frances de Chantal in 1637), the examples I've found of Saints receiving this great grace come from close to our own day. I was born in 1965. St. Anthony Mary Claret received this grace only 104 years before my birth; St. Faustina and Blessed Dina just decades before I was born; and Padre Pio, assuming he lived with Jesus' Real Presence in him between Communions until his death in 1968, experienced this miracle in my lifetime.

Why now, we might ask?

It is only relatively recently that the Church, through the pastoral mercy of Pope St. Pius X, began to recommend daily Communion for all the faithful starting as early as age seven. Then in the revised Code of Canon Law issued by St. John Paul II in 1983, the Church has allowed the faithful to receive the Blessed Sacrament *twice* a day—granted, under certain conditions, but these conditions are not very restrictive.

I have tried to look at this Eucharistic miracle from God's point of view. He is love—how can we be surprised if He, once again, stops at nothing to unite us with Himself?

But once again looking at it from our point of view, we can see that even our poor love has, in some way, the character of wanting (at least wanting) to stop at nothing.

I have a friend whose wife, when they dated, was not Catholic. She eventually became Catholic, but first, when they were courting and he explained to her our belief in the Real Presence in the Blessed Sacrament, she laughed at him and accused him of lying. When he protested that he was telling the truth, she had a convincing (or convicting, to him) objection: If, she said, you really believed this, you would be crawling on your knees to receive Him! You'd at least be going every day to receive Him. There's no way, then, given your apparent indifference, that this is true.

Well, it was true, and my friend realized that what didn't make sense was his lackadaisical attitude about the Real Presence. He became a daily communicant because he knew his future wife was absolutely right.

When we begin to realize what this gift is that God gives us in the Holy Eucharist—Our Lord: Body, Blood, Soul, and Divinity—there are two possibilities. We either quickly forget it on a practical level, or we begin to make an effort to receive Him more often, to adore Him hidden in the Host exposed in the monstrance, to make visits to Him hidden in the Host further hidden in the tabernacle.

And when, in our little strivings to be Saints, we begin to receive Him more and He begins to wake us up (as He woke Samuel), it is inevitable—hopefully!—that we fall in love with Him and want, like the Saints wanted, to be with Him as much as possible.

We are in this marvelous time of unprecedented access to Jesus in the Blessed Sacrament. We are invited to receive Him daily—and allowed to receive Him twice daily, even!

It has been the teaching of theologians (in conjunction with experimental science and our knowledge of digestion) that the

Blessed Sacrament remains within us as long as the Sacred Species—the consecrated Host—perdures, which is about fifteen minutes. Hence St. Maximilian Kolbe made a Spiritual Communion every fifteen minutes. That is, I don't know for sure if that's why he made a Spiritual Communion every fifteen minutes, but it stands to reason. He was in love with Jesus and wanted to be with Him as much and as often as possible, especially in this intense relationship of Holy Communion. But since he could receive Jesus and "keep Him" this way only once a day, that meant only fifteen minutes with Jesus' Real Presence in him. Hence his need to ask Our Lord, at fifteen minute intervals, to come back and stay, at least spiritually.

May I say, from my vantage point as a very little soul who loves but is terrible at showing it in deeds, that even for me—let alone for one who, like St. Maximilian, loved unto death—fifteen minutes is simply not enough time.

The Curé of Ars said, "We can only receive God once a day; a soul enkindled with divine love makes up for this by the desire of receiving Him every moment of the day." This is exactly what St. Thérèse desired, enkindled as she was with divine love. And if we are not feeling too enkindled, we can pray with her the Act of Oblation and ask for that very enkindling.

From another angle (though still through my little eyes), consider this: if we had any clue, even just the least bit more understanding than we have now, about what it means for Jesus to be truly present in the Blessed Sacrament, how could we ever leave Him?

I am lucky enough to have been tricked by Jesus into a once-a-week holy hour. I had made a visit one Friday morning when our parish has Eucharistic exposition and signed up to be an alternate for that hour. The "captain" of the hour was quite adamant that I need not take my obligation too seriously: she was *always* there, she said; newly retired and often there for more hours than the 11 a.m. hour that I now shared.

So, keeping up the pretence of my hectic modern life (it is simply not done to be not busy in our era), and in accord with my skewed priorities (often preferring bookstores to church, for instance), I never showed up. Until one Friday, some months later, when I not only showed up, not only discovered Jesus alone (for anyone who's ever had a holy hour, you know this is your worst fear—to find Him alone on your watch; worse than pathetic, I felt), but I also found on the sign-in sheet that Jesus and his proxy, the good man in charge of the holy hour schedule, had bumped me up to captain of the hour when I wasn't looking!

You will be relieved to know I've done much better since that day, finding a substitute when my family is on vacation, but otherwise there at my post each week. I've even had a friend join in and make it "our hour," which has been a joy.

But I mention this now because you will know, when I say next what I must say next, that I am not all that fabulous an adorer. I know the hours of falling asleep, instead of staying awake with Him. I know the hours of being wide awake, but thinking more about what's for lunch than about Whose Presence it is before Whom I sit, comfortably, in the pew.

Even the littlest souls, though, cannot always escape a consciousness of Jesus' captivating Presence. And so I have had hours—or more likely minutes—that slipped by, and too soon it was time to leave. And then even I have found myself loathe to leave Him, and saying before I left, "Jesus, come with me!" I would then console myself with the doctrine of the Indwelling Trinity, that other extraordinary "ordinary" state of the soul in grace, and content myself with knowing, however forgetfully, that Jesus in His Divine Nature would go with me into the rest of my day.

Since I have discovered Thérèse's something new, I marvel at the possibility and the sheer sensibleness of the miracle she asked for and urges us to request with her. For if we had one iota of awareness, wouldn't it hurt (excuse the expression, but I think it fits here) like hell to tear ourselves away from Him in the Blessed Sacrament?

I've come across, lately, a saying in the lives of the Saints that goes like this: "I'm happy to stay on earth as long as God wills it. After all, what more will I have in Heaven, since I have Jesus here in the Blessed Sacrament?" These were well catechized Saints, and they knew they would have the Beatific Vision in Heaven: pure, uninterrupted, eternal bliss. Their point, however, was that the joy of Heaven is in being with God, and they already have God's presence here, just as truly, in the Holy Eucharist. Although here they are with Him in the darkness of faith, and there they will see Him face to Face, still in one very important sense—that of being with God, in His presence—they already have here what awaits them there.

I want to think that way too.

In the early 1980s I went with my parents and my godmother to "the big city" to see a documentary that had come out on Mother Teresa. After the film, which moved the whole audience tremendously, I went to use the restroom in the theatre. A wealthy San Francisco socialite (so she seemed to me) was at the sink and I asked her what she thought of the movie. "Well," she said, sounding annoyed, "If I had faith like that …"

God bless her, I don't remember if she even finished the sentence, her implication being that the film hadn't moved *her* (in an identifiably positive way), because what did she have in common with Mother Teresa? That kind of life was obviously tied to that kind of faith (that degree of faith), and the poor woman couldn't even conceive of it.

I remember feeling sad for her, and as I say, may God bless her, wherever she is now. But I thought, and still think, that our attitude toward the Saints ought to be one of joy—at least gratitude that we could live on the same planet as such amazing people—and a smidgen of hope, if not bucketsful, that we could, by God's grace, imitate them just a little. While that means having gifts that only God can give, we can at least for our part desire a mustard seed version of their tremendous God-given faith.

And so, walking around this new idea, this new outrageous grace I have discovered in the lives of the Saints, and trying to view it from all perspectives, and most of all trying to comprehend how I could live it as they did, I see that my problem is fundamentally an inability to comprehend the love of the Heart of God. But I'm going to keep trying, if not to comprehend it, certainly to believe in it.

God is infinitely kinder than any of us can imagine, so it should not surprise us if we are continually beginners in this act of believing in love. In eternity we can, perhaps, move to the advanced level, but while on earth even St. Thomas considered, after having a vision of God toward the end of his life, that all he had written—and Jesus had told him he had written well— was mere straw. Which just goes to show that even the greatest among us is very small, while He is, as Thérèse told us and I love to repeat, kinder than we can ever imagine.

Chapter 8

The Universal Call to Holiness

Oh! I beg you, become a Saint. God is begging this from you.

—St. Thérèse, *Last Conversations*

Among the Saints, Thérèse is extraordinary for the lack of the extraordinary in her life. We've had over 100 years of papal endorsements and her abundant roses to make her seem awfully big to us still stuck on earth, but she was and remains unusual precisely in her littleness and we must not forget that.

I recently read the delightful account of Marcel Van, a Vietnamese boy who, in the mid-20th century, asked St. Thérèse to be his spiritual sister. She agreed, and the story of their friendship is marvelous. I highly recommend the book that has become my constant companion, Marcel Van's *Conversations*, in which he tells us what Jesus, Mary, and St. Thérèse said to him, as well as what he said to them. But especially pertinent here is how Van met St. Thérèse at the outset. He had been in the chapel of his junior seminary one night in 1942 and felt a strong inspiration to become a saint. He didn't know what to do with this inspiration: he was sure it must come from the devil because all

Saints were great, lived amidst the extraordinary favors of God, worked miracles constantly, and so on. He was convinced, then, that his desire to become a great Saint himself must be a terrible act of presumption. But fight it though he did, he could not rid himself of this desire, which seemed to come from God. He was in a painful bind.

He asked the Blessed Mother to help him sort out his confusion and ease his troubled soul, then he left the chapel for study hall.

Since he had already done his homework, he was allowed to read one of the lives of the Saints from the collection on a particular shelf. He knew many of them from previous reading, and the others were unattractive to him, mostly because they didn't have pictures. Closing his eyes and scrambling the books, he "recited a kind of magic formula to the Blessed Virgin" to guide his hand. He blindly selected *Story of a Soul.*

His reaction? "I let the book fall noisily on the pile of books, with the intention of leaving it to one side without even opening it." But then Van realized this was breaking his agreement with Our Lady, so he picked up the book again—and proceeded "to summarize her [Thérèse's] life in an amusing manner in these terms: 'Since her birth until her last breath she had many ecstasies and performed a number of miracles; she fasted on bread and water, only taking one meal a day; she spent the night in prayer and gave herself the discipline until she bled. After her death her body exhaled a very pleasant fragrance and many extraordinary things happened on her tomb...'" (*The Autobiography of Brother Marcel Van*, 568).

Van knew nothing about St. Thérèse, and after he recounts his first guess at her life (before bothering to open her book), he writes in his *Autobiography,* "O, my dear sister, you must necessarily be a saint of heroic courage to put up with the erroneous judgments that I have held on your life." For what came next?

When Van read her *Story of a Soul*, he found in Thérèse the answer he had pleaded for in the chapel. His desires for sanctity were definitely from God: here was the example he needed, a Saint who was little, like he was, and yet aspired to the heights not because of who she was, but because of who God was. Her weakness—and later Van's, and now ours—would provide the perfectly irresistible setting for God's power and merciful love.

We forget that Thérèse's message is new. We forget because, despite the vicissitudes the Church has suffered since Vatican II, one fruit of the Council has ripened to absolute perfection, assisted by Jesus' vicar, His Polish gardener, John Paul II. The universal call to holiness has become a byword—of course we are called to be Saints! I remember the talk during the 1990s, Church gossip you might call it, about whether the Pope was raising too many Saints to the altar, cheapening the process as it were, presiding at so many beatifications and canonizations that sainthood would in the future mean nothing special.

To the contrary, the Holy Father was simply placing before us every possible model God placed before him, determined to share with us our patrimony, our brothers and sisters in the Faith. He was helping us to follow the exhortation from the letter to the Hebrews: "Remember your leaders who spoke the word of God to you; consider how their lives ended, and imitate their faith" (Hebrews 13:7).

In his book *Why He is a Saint*, the postulator of John Paul II's cause begins with this anecdote:

> One day, a nun serving in the papal apartments noticed that John Paul II seemed unusually fatigued. She shared her concern with him, telling him that she was "worried about Your Holiness." "Oh, I'm worried about my holiness, too," was the pope's cheerful and immediate response. (p. 1)

Later, in a section titled "Taking Inspiration from the Saints for the Practice of Virtues," the postulator explains:

> With the intention of offering the faithful a variegated mosaic of models to imitate, John Paul II proclaimed 483 saints and 1,345 blessed during his pontificate. In two large files, which he kept in his bedroom, he had the biographies of each of those saints and blessed, and he often spent time reading and rereading them to find inspiration for the practice of the virtues. (p. 158)

Little Thérèse was the only one—among the hundreds upon hundreds who provided him with daily inspiration—that St. John Paul II named a Doctor of the Church. We might think she is numbered among the Doctors despite her littleness, but I think she would correct us and underline that it is precisely because of her littleness. As she did for Marcel Van (now a Servant of God), so she does for us: she strengthens our hope and our conviction that we too are called to be Saints.

She says, "Without showing Himself, without making His voice heard, Jesus teaches me in secret" (*Story of a Soul*, p. 189). He taught her in the same way He teaches us, through a word, often from Scripture but not always; a word heard or read at the right moment. She explains:

> Never have I heard Him speak, but I feel that He is within me at each moment; He is guiding and inspiring me with what I must say and do. I find just when I need them certain lights that I had not seen until then, and it isn't most frequently during my hours of prayer that these are most abundant but rather in the midst of my daily occupations. (*Story of a Soul*, 179)

She wouldn't have had it any other way, for as she neared the end of her life on earth, she had one extraordinary light: that she would be a model for other little souls, and therefore she didn't want to do or have anything that would alienate them—us!—and cause us to say, "Oh, but hers is not really a way I can follow; I'm a weak and often failing sinner, whereas she was a great Saint." She was way ahead of us, sure, but only in her insight that if she did anything big, or had anything extraordinary happen to her, we would give up before we had even begun to follow her.

Because of her desire to be completely imitable, she warned her sisters not to expect her body to be found incorrupt after her death (later, it wasn't). When Marie of the Trinity thought it would be lovely if Thérèse died after Communion on the Feast of Our Lady of Mount Carmel—such a beautiful death, Thérèse retorted:

> To die after Communion! On a great feastday! Oh! no this isn't how I wish to die! This would be an extraordinary grace that would discourage all the little souls, because they couldn't imitate that. They must be able to imitate everything about me! (*Thérèse of Lisieux and Marie of the Trinity*, p. 37)

When it comes back, then, to her outrageous desire and petition that Jesus would remain in her as in a tabernacle, we can conclude two things:

1. That she, unlike St. Anthony Mary Claret, St. Faustina, St. Padre Pio, St. Margaret Mary, and Blessed Dina Belanger, did not have any visible or audible assurance from Our Lord that He had answered her prayer.
2. That just as she is imitable in having no locutions or visions, she is imitable in this desire and petition.

As Marie of the Trinity, having learned her lesson well, so aptly reflected in later years, this Eucharistic miracle is thus quite fitting for little souls, "since it is a grace granted to their humble confidence and which operates in bare faith." In this clear dark night of faith, Thérèse is our model of confident assurance, of believing in God's love even to the point of folly.

And when we want signs? The beauty of Thérèse is her simplicity. She tells us to go ahead and ask, and she will send roses, and then our timid hearts will begin to believe a little more in God's love.

Another of my favorite stories about St. Thérèse comes from the "Shower of Roses" reported to the Lisieux Carmel a few years after her death. Its context is an exchange between Thérèse and Marie of the Trinity in 1897, when Thérèse was dying. Thérèse one day asked Marie, "After I die, will you abandon the little way?" Marie replied, "Surely not. I believe in it so firmly that it seems to me that even if the pope would tell me that you have been deceived, I couldn't believe it." Thérèse quickly corrected her ardent disciple, responding:

> Oh! One must believe the pope before all else. But don't be afraid that he will tell you to change the way; I won't give him time for that. Because if when I arrive in Heaven I learn that I have led you into error, I will get permission from God to return immediately and inform you. Until then, believe that my way is certain and follow it faithfully. (*Thérèse of Lisieux and Marie of the Trinity*, p. 77)

Another time, Marie recorded similar words from her novice mistress:

> If I am leading you in error with my little way of love, don't be afraid that I would let you follow it for very long. I would appear to you soon in order to tell you to take another route. But if I don't return, believe in the truth of my words: one can never have too much confidence in God, who is so powerful and so merciful! One receives from Him quite as much as one hopes for! (Ibid.)

Thérèse, however, was never one to let the grass—even celestial grass—grow under her feet. Of course she didn't need to return to inform anyone her way was false, but neither did she make her sisters wait for the popes to tell them that it was trustworthy. Her mission is to make Love loved, and quickly. Why not come down to tell those following her Little Way that it was safe? After all, within two years of her death there were already thousands embarking on this way, thanks to the first printings of *Story of a Soul.*

Here is where our Shower of Roses story comes in. The Lisieux Carmel received an increasing stream, eventually a torrent of letters in the years following Thérèse's entrance into Heaven (during the World War, despite the postal difficulties, the number mounted to about 500 letters a day). Some of the letters asked for miracles through the intercession of Sister Thérèse, others sent thanks for miracles already obtained. In 1910, one of these thanksgiving letters came from a Carmelite monastery in Gallipoli, Italy.

The Mother Superior wrote that her Carmel had been in distressed circumstances—destitute, really—when, the community having publicly read *Story of a Soul* and begun a triduum begging Thérèse's intercession, the Mother Superior had a dream that a Carmelite touched her on the shoulder and explained, "The Good God makes use of the inhabitants of Heaven, as well as those of earth, in order to assist His servants. Here are 500 francs, with which you will pay the debt of your community." Since it was against the rule to keep money in the prioress' cell, the "young Carmelite nun, whose veil and robes shone with a brightness from paradise that served to light up our way," led Mother Carmela to the parlor where they put the money in a wooden box. Mother Carmela thought the nun was the great St. Teresa, but the visitor, caressing her affectionately, said, "No, I am not our holy Mother. I am the servant of God, Sister Thérèse of Lisieux."

When Thérèse slowly withdrew, the priories called out, "Wait! You might mistake your way." To which Thérèse replied with a Heavenly smile, "No, no. My way is sure, and I am not mistaken in following it" (*Soeur Thérèse of Lisieux, The Little Flower of Jesus*, p. 340).

The prioress awoke, and when she later went to the parlor accompanied by two of her Sisters, they discovered the miraculous 500 francs in the wooden box.

In subsequent months, Sister Thérèse (not yet beatified, but in Heaven nonetheless) visited the monastery with more funds, and the Bishop became involved. He witnessed a miracle of money appearing in a sealed envelope. His response? "He saw a higher purpose in the miracle—the confirmation, namely, of the Saint's remark: 'My Way is a Sure one' which he had written on the sealed envelope before the miracle occurred."

I love this story because it affirms Thérèse's very personal interest in those left on earth. Marie of the Trinity wrote, after Thérèse's entrance into Heaven:

> I feel her even closer to me than when we were together. When she was on earth, I had to endure sharing her with many other people, but now she is with me entirely and I don't have to share her anymore. I think this is the privilege of all those who are part of the legion of "little souls," of whom she is the queen. (*Thérèse of Lisieux and Marie of the Trinity*, pp. 43-44)

Thérèse continues to reach out to us, to come down, to make sure we don't fall off her Little Way, to guide us back when we do. And yet all these years later, we don't have to depend only on her word, her nearness, her "coming down" to prove to us her way is sure. As she told Marie of the Trinity, "One must believe the pope before all else," and not merely one, but ten popes have assured us of the truth of her teaching.

Here is Céline's reaction to the first public acknowledgment given to Thérèse's doctrine by a pope. Céline wrote:

> I have never experienced such great and deep joy as I did on August 14, 1921, when Pope Benedict XV made his papal announcement, which enthusiastic telegrams told us had extolled 'the little Way of Spiritual Childhood' as well as the heroicity of Thérèse's virtues. That was the victory I had desired without daring to hope that it would be so complete. The beatification and canonization themselves did not bring me as intense a happiness. (*Céline*, p. 111)

And what was it Pope Benedict XV said that so overjoyed Céline? Having promulgated the Decree on the Heroicity of the Virtues, he responded to thanks offered by the Bishops of Bayeux and Lisieux, and in his *allocutio* he explained:

> It is not difficult to identify the merits of this spiritual childhood both in what it excludes as in what it supposes ... It excludes the presumption of achieving a supernatural end by human means...And, on the other hand, it supposes living faith in the existence of God; supposes practical homage to His power and mercy; it supposes trusting recourse to the providence of Him from whom we can obtain grace both to avoid every evil and achieve every good ... We hope that the secret of the sanctity of Sister Thérèse of the Child Jesus remains hidden to no one. (*30 Giorni*, "The Popes and Little Teresa of the Child Jesus," Giovanni Ricciardi)

Pope Benedict XV gives us wise words of guidance in what we can suppose, as well as what we must exclude, while following Thérèse's Little Way. The Pope points out that her way "excludes the presumption of achieving a supernatural end by human means," while yet "it supposes trusting recourse to the providence of Him from whom we can obtain grace both to avoid every evil and achieve every good."

Thérèse urges us—and the Pope's endorsement seals the deal—to place our trust in God from whom we can obtain grace to "achieve every good."

This good of Jesus' abiding Real Presence in the soul between Communions is a good I never would have dreamed up on my own. Nor do I think that on my own I would have stumbled over it—and noticed it, or thought it had anything to do with me—in the lives of the Saints, where it has been hidden, for the most part, like a light under a bushel basket. It took Thérèse's childlike audacity, her "You promised!" to God our loving Father, and the witness of Marie of the Trinity in experiencing this great grace too, to draw my attention to the possibilities.

Pope Pius XII, when his turn came to endorse Thérèse's doctrine, had this to say, on the occasion of the consecration of the Basilica of Lisieux:

> Thérèse learned at her father's knee the treasures of indulgence and compassion that are concealed in the heart of the Lord! God is the Father whose arms are constantly outstretched to His children. Why not respond to this gesture?" (*30 Giorni*, "The Popes and Little Teresa of the Child Jesus," Giovanni Ricciardi)

And how do we respond to God's outstretched arms? Thérèse would have us respond with surrender and gratitude, by believing in God's infinite love for us. She wants us to have pity on Him, to satiate His thirst by letting Him love us, by letting ourselves be loved. He has gone to such lengths to find us, to save us, to draw us to Himself. But there is more He can do, and Love will leave nothing undone.

We can wait until Heaven to let Him love us completely, but sometimes that feels like a terribly long time to make Him wait—as Scripture tells us and Thérèse mentions in the Act, for Him a single day is like a thousand years (and occasionally for us, too, a day is like a thousand years). Surely that's an awfully long time for us to wait, for us to put Him off. Come with me, then, won't you? Thérèse is reaching out to grab our hands—let's allow our hands to be caught, and let's run with her, deeper into Love. She wants us to become Saints with her; she is insistent, and she insists that it won't be hard.

Unfortunately, when it comes to scaling these heights of sanctity, we aren't all that successful. Thérèse was a very bright girl, pretty, beloved, but she saw this in herself too, this inability to become a saint, and she faced it head on. She acknowledged that there was no way she could do it by her own power, and so she decided to abandon herself into God's arms, like He had suggested in the Gospels.

At the very beginning of this book I placed the following quotation from Chapter 11 of St. Matthew's Gospel:

At that time Jesus said: I give praise to You, Father, Lord of Heaven and earth, for although You have hidden these things from the wise and the learned You have revealed them to the little ones. Yes, Father, for such was Your gracious will. (Mt 11: 25-26)

Well the thing about an epigraph—the quote that opens a book or a chapter—is that it doesn't work if it's too long, so I had to leave out what comes next, but what comes next in Matthew's Gospel is the perfect antidote to our resistance to letting go. For there, Jesus says:

Come to Me, all you who labor and are burdened, and I will give you rest. Take my yoke upon you, and learn from Me, for I am gentle and humble of heart; and you will find rest for your souls. For My yoke is easy, and My burden light. (Mt 11:28-30)

St. Thérèse loved this passage, and what amazes me is that all the verses together, from Jesus' praise of the Father to His invitation that we rest in Him, are so completely fulfilled in her.

She is the little one—that's how she identified herself and how the Church has identified her—to whom it pleased the Father to reveal the things He had hidden from the wise. And what were these things He revealed to her? Jesus' gentleness, His meekness and humility of heart, and His promise that if only we will come to Him, surrender, abandon ourselves and all our cares to Him, we will find rest at last. This is the story of Thérèse's soul down to the last word. She said toward the end of her exile:

> As for me, with the exception of the Gospels, I no longer find anything in books. The Gospels are enough. I listen with delight to these words of Jesus which tell me all I must do: "Learn of Me for I am meek and humble of heart"; then I'm at peace, according to His sweet promise: "and you will find rest for your little souls." (*Last Conversations*, p. 44)

Mother Agnes comments that when Thérèse quoted Jesus' invitation, "she added the word 'little' to Our Lord's words, thus giving them even more charm: 'And you will find rest for your *little* souls.'"

I've acknowledged our indebtedness to Marie of the Sacred Heart and Marie of the Trinity. We've seen how much we owe Céline too. Now it's time to thank Pauline—for as Mother Agnes, she not only had Thérèse, at their sister Marie's insistence, write her childhood memories (which became the first part of *Story of a Soul*), and later gained Mother Marie de Gonzague's request for Thérèse to write her monastery memories (which became the third part of *Story of a Soul*), but she also did us the huge favor of asking her little sister, point blank, to "explain what she meant by 'remaining a little child before God.'" And because

Pauline made sure to write down everything Thérèse said in the last months of her life, we have the answer. Thérèse said:

> It is to recognize our nothingness, to expect everything from God as a little child expects everything from its father; it is to be disquieted about nothing, and not to be set on gaining our living. Even among the poor, they give the child what is necessary, but as soon as he grows up, his father no longer wants to feed him and says: 'Work now, you can take care of yourself.'
>
> It was so as not to hear this that I never wanted to grow up, feeling that I was incapable of making my living, the eternal life of Heaven. I've always remained little, therefore, having no other occupation but to gather flowers, the flowers of love and sacrifice, and of offering them to God in order to please Him.
>
> To be little is not attributing to oneself the virtues that one practices, believing oneself capable of anything, but to recognize that God places this treasure in the hands of His little child to be used when necessary; but it remains always God's treasure. Finally, it is not to become discouraged over one's faults, for children fall often, but they are too little to hurt themselves very much. (*Last Conversations,* pp. 138-139)

This, then, is what Thérèse intends when she encourages us to surrender to God, to entirely dedicate ourselves to Him, to abandon ourselves into His arms. We must simply acknowledge that He is the source of all our goods, exterior and interior. When confronted with our weakness, we don't need to fret, since of ourselves we are nothing; and when, now and then, we find ourselves happily virtuous, we can rejoice in our Father's goodness, for He has shared with us some of His treasures: love, patience, fortitude and the rest.

Thérèse identified Jesus' arms as the elevator that would lift us to holiness and Heaven, but if we are faced with stairs, she has another helpful image. She told Marie of the Trinity:

> You make me think of the very little child who starts to hold herself up but does not yet know how to walk. Wanting absolutely to climb to the top of the stairs to find her mother again, she lifts her little foot to finally climb the first step. Useless labor! She always falls without making any advance. Okay! Consent to be this little child … On the happy day when Jesus will Himself come down to carry you away in His arms, will you be more advanced by having clambered up five or six steps by your own strength? Is it more difficult for Jesus to take you from the bottom rather than from the middle of the stairs? (*Thérèse of Lisieux and Marie of the Trinity*, pp. 79-80)

Thérèse explains that He is very pleased by our good will, by our raising our foot to "clamber up the stairs of holiness." She smilingly tells us, "You will not even get to the first rung, but God asks nothing of you except your good will. From the top of the stairs, He looks down at you with love. Soon, won over by your ineffective efforts, He will come down Himself and take you into His arms … " (p. 80).

Bishop Guy Gaucher, in his book *John and Thérèse*, quotes St. John of the Cross describing in a similar way this same essential truth: we must depend upon God Himself to lift us to the heights of sanctity. Thérèse's holy Father in Carmel wrote:

> The soul thereby imitates children and their mothers carrying them in their arms so as to spare them the trouble of walking … The soul advances more rapidly than if she walked herself, also when she doesn't feel it, because God carries her in His arms … the soul then has only

one thing to do. This is to remain in the hands of God and to abandon herself to her Father's conduct with total confidence. (*John and Thérèse*, p. 156)

When Thérèse begins her Act of Oblation, she states in the first paragraph her desires for sanctity, but concludes: "I desire, in a word, to be a Saint, but I feel my powerlessness and I beg You, O my God! to be Yourself my *Sanctity!*"

And then she goes on, beloved child of our loving Father, to remind Him of His promises. He has promised to give her whatever she asks, so she asks Him to stay in her as in a tabernacle. Is He not all-powerful? In fact, Thérèse had understood God's omnipotence, particularly with respect to the Holy Eucharist, from a very young age. Her mother, now St. Zelie, died when Thérèse was four, but in *Story of a Soul* Thérèse quotes the following from a letter her mother wrote to Pauline in May of 1877 (thus, the incident recounted occurred when Thérèse was four):

It's true that she [Thérèse] has very rare answers for one her age; she surpasses Céline in this who is twice her age. Céline said the other day: "How is it that God can be present in a small host?" The little one said: "That is not surprising, God is all powerful." "What does all powerful mean?" "It means He can do what He wants!" (*Story of a Soul*, p. 27)

Years later, Thérèse had a new suspicion of what He wanted. She knew what He wanted by reflecting on what she wanted. She reminds Him in the Act, "I know, O my God! that the more You want to give, the more You make us desire. I am certain then that You will grant my desires." As He is present in the Host—Body, Blood, Soul and Divinity—so she wants Him to be present in her, never separating Himself from her. What better way for her to ensure, to fulfill completely (and we might even say literally), her idea of remaining a child in God's arms? And remaining in this union with Jesus, she illustrates perfectly St. John of the Cross' teaching: "The soul advances more rapidly than if she walked herself, also when she doesn't feel it, because God carries her in His arms."

At four she told her sister about His presence in the small consecrated Host, "That is not surprising. God is all powerful." She had the same reaction eighteen years later when her novice Marie of the Trinity "experienced in a very tangible way the presence of the Eucharistic Jesus" in her heart after making her Offering to Merciful Love. Marie tells us, "I confided this to Sister Thérèse of the Child Jesus, who was not at all surprised and answered me simply: 'Is God not omnipotent? If we so desire, it would not be difficult for Him to make His sacramental presence in our souls remain from one Communion to the next." And as we have seen, Thérèse goes on to assure Marie that this is what He is doing in her, namely, granting her requests, granting this request. "You will not always enjoy these feelings," Thérèse warns her, but then reassures, "but their effects will be no less real. One receives from God as much as one hopes for" (*Thérèse of Lisieux and Marie of the Trinity*, p. 70).

There is an argument here. We are called to be Saints. The popes have told us this, and they have repeatedly proposed to us a sure way to fulfill this calling: by following St. Thérèse on her Little Way of Spiritual Childhood. In explaining her Little Way, she tells us we need only abandon ourselves into God's arms, knowing that He will give us good desires and then will Himself fulfill these desires. It is not our job to climb all those flights of stairs to Heaven. For our part we simply keep lifting our foot, and trusting Him to carry us soon. To be Saints, we need to trust Him to make us Saints.

I remember asking a holy and elderly Jesuit how I could become a Saint. He was holy, so I thought he would know the answer. He was elderly, so I thought I had better ask him right away. He looked at me after I had asked him point blank, "How do I become a Saint?" and he said, to my astonishment and dismay, "*You* can't become a Saint!"

I suppose in a way I wasn't surprised—a light coating of the dust of Jansenism still clings to me—but I wasn't expecting this. Father looked serious, and this was certainly bad news.

Then he broke into a grin. "*You* can't become a Saint," he repeated, and then explained, "Only Jesus can make you a Saint!"

He can, and He will. And He will leave nothing undone. Which is why He's constantly coming up with new ways to charm us, to draw us, to scoop us up in His embrace so that once we're safe in His arms, He can lift us up to His Father.

Here is an example from the last hundred years. In the 1930s, Jesus told a Polish nun, "Paint an image," and He described the image carefully, even as the nun beheld Him under the very appearance. Then he insisted she have an inscription written across the picture—"Jesus, I trust in You."

The nun wasn't an artist, but by God's providence, she found one. Not surprisingly, he couldn't paint Jesus' face as beautifully as she'd seen it. She had him keep trying, but one day, as she wept over the unlikeness, Jesus explained to her that she shouldn't worry: the grace of the picture would not be in its colors or perfect likeness or beauty, but in the meaning of the image of His Divine Mercy.

Jesus had lots of other instructions for this dear young nun, and the story of how He brought about all He asked of her and through her would make another book. We can content ourselves here with noting that three years after Pope John Paul II elevated Thérèse to the level of Doctor, he proclaimed this nun, Faustina Kowalska, a Saint, and he instituted Divine Mercy Sunday. And behind Faustina's sanctity, behind this new universal Feast are these simple words: Jesus, I trust in You.

Along with the image and words that Jesus gave us through Faustina, He also gave us a prayer to say: the Divine Mercy Chaplet. Our Lord was obviously determined to give us every possible means to fight evil and promote good.

I say "obviously" because St. Anthony Mary Claret reports that Jesus told him, too, of important prayers to say. On August 27, 1861, the day after granting Anthony "the great grace of retaining the sacramental species," Our Lord enlightened him "in regard to the three evils menacing Spain, which are ... the decrease of the Catholic spirit, the Republic, and Communism," and gave him three remedies to counteract the evils: "The Trisagion Ss. Trinitatis, devotion to the Blessed Sacrament, and devotion to the Holy Rosary" (*The Autobiography of St. Anthony Mary Claret*, pp. 180-181).

St. Anthony writes, "The Trisagion is to be said daily." Fortunately for me, his editor provided a handy bracketed explanation: "This is 'the thrice-holy hymn' found in the Divine Office and the Good Friday liturgy: 'Holy God, holy Mighty One, holy Immortal One, have mercy on us.'" And more fortunately still, Jesus didn't wait for us to discover this prayer hidden in St. Anthony's memoir—He told us more directly, through his dear Polish Saints, Faustina and John Paul II, to say it as frequently as we say our Divine Mercy chaplet.

This is a God who knows we are very small children. He will raise up for us as many Saints as we need, provide as many devotions, remind us with infinite gentleness and unending patience what exactly it is we need to do.

And now—not 100 years ago, not "near our own time," not twenty years ago even, but today—today Jesus is giving us a new way of complete union with Him, a new way to abandon ourselves into His arms, a new way to follow Thérèse's Little Way.

Thérèse needed to keep it simple, and so, that she might keep the message in mind that Jesus brought us from our Father, she focused on His love, first and foremost. And as Mother Agnes testified in the Process, "When she thought of God's all-powerful love, she had no doubts about anything."

We may have to think for a very long time about God's all-powerful love before we have no doubts about anything. And while I highly recommend thinking about His love as often as we can, there is a shorter on-ramp to the Little Way. We can ask Thérèse to help us, as she helped Céline, Marie of the Sacred Heart, and Marie of the Trinity, to make our offering to Merciful Love.

We can recite with her the Act of Oblation, and when we get to the part where we ask Jesus to remain in us as in a tabernacle, we, like the little children we are, simply mean what we say. Is He not all-powerful? He can do it, and the lives of the Saints show us that He has.

He continues to raise up new Saints to show us how various and unending are the signs of His love, and how attractive the manifestations of His perfection. As I write, we are approaching a day I've been waiting for a long time: the canonization of Blessed Elizabeth of the Trinity. When you read this, she'll officially be Saint Elizabeth of the Trinity, and she, too, has a message for us.

Elizabeth had a one track mind. When she discovered, as a young girl, that her name meant "house of God," she was elated because she had already been attracted to the mystery of God dwelling within her. She then devoted her brief life (she died in 1906 at age 26) to entering within herself to spend time with God there, keeping Him company, loving Him, and especially letting Him love her.

Elizabeth was born when St. Thérèse was seven years old, and though they never knew each other during Thérèse's lifetime—Elizabeth was only eight when Thérèse entered the convent at fifteen—not long after Thérèse died, Elizabeth read the first edition of *Story of a Soul*.

Elizabeth, like Thérèse, was French. She, too, became a Carmelite. And as I said, she too has a message for us, a message she left in a letter to her Mother Superior to be read after Elizabeth's death. Now that God has raised up Elizabeth as a friend, exemplar, and intercessor for the whole Church, I think it's important that we take her message personally. It too is very simple, and fits perfectly with the message of this book. St. Elizabeth tells us:

> You are uncommonly loved, loved by that love of preference that the Master had here below for some and which brought them so far. He does not say to you as to Peter: "Do you love Me more than these?" Listen to what He tells you: "Let yourself be loved more than these! That is, without fearing that any obstacle will be a hindrance to it, for I am free to pour out My love on whom I wish! 'Let yourself be loved more than these' is your vocation. It is in being faithful to it that you will make Me happy for you will magnify the power of My love."

"How simple it is for you," Elizabeth continues, "and that is exactly what makes it so luminous! Let yourself be loved more than the others; that explains everything and prevents the soul from being surprised" (*Elizabeth of the Trinity, Complete Works, Volume One*, p. 179).

We have asked ourselves, in the course of this book, whether it is possible to believe that Jesus would grant us the grace of His remaining in us as in a tabernacle. Following St. Thérèse, I've been using every available means to assure you that really, God loves us so much that He is quite likely to want to give us—you and me—this inestimable grace.

We've seen that He has given this gift of Himself to some of the great Saints, and the greatest Saint of modern times assured one of her friends, Marie of the Trinity, that He had given it to her, Marie, an unworthy humble novice, too. Thérèse even went so far as to say that God wanted to lavish this grace, and many more, on all little souls who would offer themselves to His Merciful Love.

If it helps you to think this grace is the mark of a preferential love, I won't argue—I'm sure it is. But don't try to get out of being loved by saying you're not one whom He prefers. With St. Elizabeth, I would have to repeat that "Let yourself be loved more than these" is your vocation. And with St. Thérèse, I would like to tell all little souls—that is, all souls—how kind Jesus is (much kinder than we can imagine), and to what infinite lengths He will go to find us and keep us close to His Heart.

In conclusion, I'm absolutely positive about one thing: Thérèse wants us to share her joy in God's love. She found the fullness of that joy in her surrender to His Merciful Love, offering herself so that the floodtides of His infinite tenderness could overflow into her soul, and she invites us to make the Act of Oblation (which you will find at the end of this book) with her.

As for me, I can imitate her in no better way than to laugh at myself for trying to tell all little souls how unspeakable is His condescension. And so, abandoning the stairs for the elevator, I repeat with St. Thérèse: "O Jesus, can You not reveal Your secrets of Love to others? Yes, I know it, and I beg You to do it."

Epilogue

To Jesus through Mary

He that made me, rested in my tabernacle.

—Ecclesiasticus 24:12

At the outset, I explained that my discovery of "something new" began when I heard a talk by Fr. Michael Gaitley, author of *33 Days to Morning Glory*, a book on Marian consecration. I mentioned, too, that Fr. Gaitley's talk the day I heard him was on another book he'd written, this one on St. Thérèse, but more particularly on consecration to Divine Mercy according to the spirit of her Act of Oblation.

I've been reflecting on that progression in Father Gaitley's writings, a progression I've experienced in my own spiritual life, a progression best expressed by the traditional formula "To Jesus through Mary."

I've emphasized Thérèse's desire to be imitable in all things, and recently I noticed that she too followed this classic sequence, and in such a way that she becomes, again, our model and guiding star.

In her Act, after offering God the infinite treasures of Jesus' merits and then all the merits of the Saints and Angels, she says: "Finally, I offer You, O Blessed Trinity! the Love and merits of the Blessed Virgin, my dear Mother. It is to her I abandon my offering, begging her to present it to You."

Only then, after committing her offering to the Blessed Mother, does Thérèse launch into her petition asking Jesus to remain in her as in a tabernacle. This movement from Mary to Jesus is familiar; it is reminiscent of the manner in which Thérèse prepares herself for Holy Communion. She wrote in *Story of a Soul*:

> When I am preparing for Holy Communion, I picture my soul as a piece of land and I beg the Blessed Virgin to remove from it any rubbish that would prevent it from being free; then I ask her to set up a huge tent worthy of Heaven, adorning it with her own jewelry; finally, I invite all the Angels and Saints to come and conduct a magnificent concert there. It seems to me that when Jesus descends into my heart He is content to find Himself so well received and I, too, am content. All this, however, does not prevent both distractions and sleepiness from visiting me, but at the end of the thanksgiving when I see that I've made it so badly I make a resolution to be thankful all through the rest of the day. (pp. 172-173)

It is not surprising, then, that Thérèse takes a moment to invite Mary's assistance before she requests the Eucharist's abiding presence in her soul—we might say it is a habitual movement for her. But sometimes habit is unconscious, and we should not think there is anything unconscious or *pro forma* about the way Thérèse moves from entrusting her offering to Our Lady and begging her to present it to the Blessed Trinity, to then freely asking for everything her heart desires. She has two very good reasons for the order of her words here, for turning the entire offering over to Mary before getting specific in her requests.

First, as she told her sister Marie of the Sacred Heart:

> When we address ourselves to the Saints, they make us wait a little, and we feel that they have to go and present their request; but whenever I ask a favor from the Blessed Virgin, I receive immediate help. Haven't you ever noticed this? Try it yourself, and you'll see. (*Last Conversations*, p. 235)

By abandoning her offering to Our Lady, Thérèse ensured that there would be no delay in her prayer reaching God, and her petitions would be immediately answered.

If, that is, they were pleasing to God, for this is her second reason for going to Jesus through Mary: she wants to make sure that her requests will delight Him. To her sister Pauline (Mother Agnes), Thérèse explained a few months before she died:

> Asking the Blessed Virgin for something is not the same thing as asking God. She really knows what is to be done about my little desires, whether or not she must speak about them to God. So it's up to her to see that God is not forced to answer me, to allow Him to do everything He pleases. (*Last Conversations*, p. 55)

O adorable and considerate Thérèse! We have seen the force of her argument requesting Him to remain in her as in a tabernacle—she has Him in a corner (He promised He would give whatever she asked, and is He not all-powerful?)—and yet she refuses to force His loving hand. She is certain that He will grant her desires ... and so, all the more imperative to place her offering in the custody of the Blessed Virgin, her most dear Mother, who will know when and if she should speak to God about Thérèse's petitions. If for some reason unforeseen by the little child, her

Father would not take great delight in granting this or that petition, she knows her Mother would not speak to Him, and thus He would be left free, not constrained by His promises or His beloved child's arguments.

We cannot do better than follow Thérèse in the trustful surrender of our dearest hopes to Our Blessed Mother. By this entrustment to Mary of ourselves and all our petitions—especially this new one Thérèse desires us to make with her—we know we will be answered speedily, but even more importantly, in the manner that brings most delight to the Blessed Trinity.

This doesn't change our fundamental outlook. Since God is our loving Father, our dearest Brother, our best friend and the spouse of our souls, we have every reason to think, with little Thérèse, that what delights Him is to make wondrous gifts which infinitely surpass our immense desires. But trusting Mary with our prayers reminds us of the main goal Thérèse wants us to share. As she prays in the Act, "I want to work for Your *Love alone* with the one purpose of pleasing You, consoling Your Sacred Heart, and saving souls who will love You eternally." Who better than Our Lady to know what will please Her Son, console His Sacred Heart, and help save souls— the souls of her own children, no less, since Jesus bequeathed us all to her when He hung on the cross.

Thérèse had originally told God her desires were infinite, but she wanted her prayer approved by the Church, so at her request Mother Agnes showed the Act of Oblation to a theologian. His only correction was that Thérèse replace the word "infinite" (in speaking of her desires) with the word "immense." She was sorry to change the word, but obedient and grateful that the rest of the Offering was approved.

Thérèse, the mischievous but obedient child with desires beyond telling, still got her wish to express her infinite desires to God, for at the end of the Act, after making the "offering proper," she prays, "I want, O my Beloved, at each beat of my heart to renew this offering to You an infinite number of times ..." Even merely "immense" desires, if expressed an infinite number of times (with each heart beat, no less) multiply to Thérèse's original infinity.

Let's not worry if our desires don't feel infinite, perhaps not even immense. Knowing her children's hearts as she does, the Blessed Mother will take the sincerity of our petitions into account, and she will know how to increase our paltry desires, if need be. As for Thérèse, after all her talk of the importance and meaning of desires, she was adamant in her response to Marie of the Sacred Heart. We have seen that when Marie expressed her concern that these impressive desires were what marked Thérèse out as a candidate for sanctity, while her own absence of desires proved she could not follow her saintly sister's way, Thérèse did not hesitate to respond with more encouragement than ever. "I beg you," she tells us as she tells Marie,

> Understand that to love Jesus, to be His *victim of love*, the weaker one is, without desires or virtues, the more suited one is for the workings of this consuming and transforming Love ... Oh! How I would like to be able to make you understand what I feel! ... It is confidence and nothing but confidence that must lead us to Love ... Since we see the way, let us run together. Yes, I feel it, Jesus wills to give us the same graces, He wills to give us His Heaven *gratuitously*. (*Letters*, pp. 999-1000; Letter 197)

We are not worthy of this gratuitous Heaven—which is why He wills to give it to us *gratis*. But as our little Saint told the novice Marie of the Trinity, it is enough that we know we are unworthy.

Since we see the way, let us run together, together with Thérèse, through Mary, to Jesus. And let us not be afraid to ask Him to remain in us, too, as in a tabernacle, for it is confidence and nothing but confidence that must lead us to Love.

Appendix I

Act of Oblation to Merciful Love

J.M.J.T.

*Offering of Myself as a Victim of Holocaust to
the Merciful Love of the Good God*

O my God! Most Blessed Trinity, I desire to *Love* You and make
You *Loved*, to work for the glory of Holy Church by saving souls
on earth and liberating those suffering in purgatory. I desire to
accomplish Your will perfectly and to reach the degree of glory
You have prepared for me in Your Kingdom. I desire, in a word,
to be a Saint, but I feel my helplessness and I beg You, O my
God! to be Yourself my *Sanctity*!

Since You loved me so much as to give me Your only Son as
my Savior and my Spouse, the infinite treasures of His merits
are mine. I offer them to You with gladness, begging You to
look upon me only in the Face of Jesus and in His Heart burning with *Love*.

I offer You, too, all the merits of the Saints (in Heaven and on
earth), their acts of *Love*, and those of the Holy Angels. Finally,

I offer You, *O Blessed Trinity!* the *Love* and merits of the *Blessed Virgin, my dear Mother.* It is to her I abandon my offering, begging her to present it to You.

Her Divine Son, my *Beloved* Spouse, told us in the days of His mortal life: *"Whatsoever you ask the Father in My name He will give it to you!"* I am certain, then, that You will grant my desires; I know, O my God! that *the more You want to give, the more You make us desire.* I feel in my heart immense desires and it is with confidence I ask You to come and take possession of my soul. Ah! I cannot receive Holy Communion as often as I desire, but, Lord, are You not *All-Powerful?* Remain in me as in a tabernacle and never separate Yourself from Your little victim.

I want to console You for the ingratitude of the wicked, and I beg of You to take away my freedom to displease You. If through weakness I sometimes fall, may Your *Divine Glance* cleanse my soul immediately, consuming all my imperfections like the fire that transforms everything into itself.

I thank You, O my God! for all the graces You have granted me, especially the grace of making me pass through the crucible of suffering. It is with joy I shall contemplate You on the Last Day carrying the scepter of Your Cross. Since You deigned to give me a share in this very precious Cross, I hope in Heaven to resemble You and to see shining in my glorified body the sacred stigmata of Your Passion.

After earth's Exile, I hope to go and enjoy You in the Fatherland, but I do not want to lay up merits for Heaven. I want to work for Your *Love alone* with the one purpose of pleasing You, consoling Your Sacred Heart, and saving souls who will love You eternally.

In the evening of this life, I shall appear before You with empty hands, for I do not ask You, Lord, to count my works. All our justice is stained in Your eyes. I wish, then, to be clothed in your own *Justice* and to receive from Your *Love* the eternal possession of *Yourself.* I want no other *Throne*, no other *Crown* but *You*, my *Beloved!*

Time is nothing in Your eyes, and a single day is like a thousand years. You can, then, in one instant prepare me to appear before You.

In order to live in one single act of perfect Love, I OFFER MYSELF AS A VICTIM OF HOLOCAUST TO YOUR MERCIFUL LOVE, asking You to consume me incessantly, allowing the waves of *infinite tenderness* shut up within You to overflow into my soul, and that thus I may become a *Martyr* of Your *Love*, O my God!

May this martyrdom, after having prepared me to appear before You, finally cause me to die and may my soul take its flight without any delay into the eternal embrace of *Your Merciful Love.*

I want, O my *Beloved*, at each beat of my heart to renew this offering to You an infinite number of times, until the shadows having disappeared I may be able to tell You of my *Love* in an *Eternal Face to Face!*

Appendix II

A Brief Biography of St. Thérèse of Lisieux

Thérèse Martin was born into a Catholic family in Alencon, a small village in France, on January 2, 1873. She was the baby, and quite a beloved baby, as she was the youngest of five living sisters who had, with their good parents Louis and Zelie, already lost two baby boys and two little girls by the time Thérèse came along. These "lost" babies were part of the family, and in fact provided Thérèse with a lesson in the friendship of the Saints when she was a young teen suffering from scruples. They interceded, at her request, and brought her a world of relief and happiness.

But long before that miracle, when Thérèse was only four years old her mother Zelie, a lace maker and a Saint, died of breast cancer. Her father Louis (also a Saint) moved the family to Lisieux, to live near Zelie's brother Isadore Guerin and his wife and their two daughters.

At their mother's death, Thérèse's oldest sisters, Marie and Pauline, took over the "motherhood" of Thérèse and her sister (older by three years) Céline. Between these two oldest and two youngest sisters was Léonie, the ugly duckling and odd one out. The lovely thing about Léonie is that, thanks to Thérèse's intercession and Léonie's perseverance along the Little Way, she eventually grew into a swan, and her cause for sainthood is now pending.

Meanwhile, according to God's mysterious timing, a few years after Zelie's death Pauline entered the nearby cloistered Carmelite monastery, leaving Thérèse once more feeling bereft. Within months, ten-year-old Thérèse, sensitive and broken hearted, suffered a frightening and mysterious illness, but after seven weeks was healed miraculously by the Blessed Mother, to whom her family had been praying. The family had a large statue of Mary, which had been very dear to Zelie, and at the moment of Thérèse's healing, she looked to the statue. Our Lady smiled upon her, and she was cured.

When she was fourteen, a year after Marie had followed Pauline into the monastery, Thérèse discerned that her long desire to become, like her older sisters, a Carmelite nun was not for "someday" but had an urgency that inspired her to ask her dear father if she could enter by fifteen. Her father generously acquiesced. It was then one trial after another and even a face to face plea at the feet of Pope Leo XIII in Rome (followed by a period of waiting) before Thérèse "finally" entered the Carmel in April of 1888, when she was slightly over fifteen years old.

Two months later her saintly father began exhibiting signs of dementia. He had offered not only his daughters, but himself also to Almighty God and God took him up on the offer. Over the next six years, with Céline and Léonie caring for him, as well as the religious sisters at a mental institution where he spent three years, he experienced an illness and death both excruciating and holy. Thérèse and her sisters called his suffering their "great trial," but also their "great treasure," and found in it a way to grow closer to Jesus.

Thérèse's persistent desire, after her own entry into Carmel, was that her soul-mate Céline should heed Jesus' call and enter the monastery also. After their father's death, and thanks to a miracle due to his intercession, Céline entered, and after Céline, their cousin Marie Guerin entered as well. Thus four of the five

Martin sisters, and one of their two Guerin cousins, ended up ensconced in the Carmel of Lisieux.

Thérèse, despite her young age—and her age was always young, for she died at 24—served as the mistress of novices at the Carmel (in obedience, though always "unofficially"). This meant that over a period of four years, she guided and taught a small group of beginning sisters, all but one of them older than she was. For part of the time, her sister Céline and her cousin Marie were among her novices. Another novice to whom she became especially spiritually close was a young Parisian, Marie of the Trinity (not to be confused with Thérèse's older sister, Marie of the Sacred Heart).

One night in late 1894, Thérèse's sister Marie of the Sacred Heart had the idea that Thérèse should write her childhood memories. Marie suggested this to their sister Pauline, who was now Mother Agnes, the Mother Superior of the monastery, and when Thérèse laughed, Marie got Mother Agnes to ask Thérèse to write out of obedience. Thérèse obeyed and wrote.

In Holy Week of 1896, four months after handing her copybook of childhood memories to Mother Agnes, Thérèse coughed up blood, the first sign of what turned out to be a fatal case of tuberculosis. For the next eighteen months she suffered a trial of faith (the dark night, as her holy Father St. John of the Cross called it), kept a smile on her face most of the time (which smile would later be a great inspiration for her namesake Saint Teresa of Calcutta), and suffered the increasing ravages of TB.

In the summer of 1897, Thérèse's sister Pauline, no longer prioress, asked the current Superior, Mother Marie de Gonzague, to have Thérèse write more of her memories—those of her religious life, since they would need "something to send" as an obituary to the other Carmels after Thérèse died. Mother Marie agreed, and again out of obedience Thérèse wrote. The compilation of her earlier memories and these, plus a reflection written for her sister Marie of the Sacred Heart, formed the book we now know as *Story of a Soul*.

For the last five months of Thérèse's life, Pauline also made sure to have all of Thérèse's "last conversations," her comments from her bed in the infirmary, written down. Pauline herself (who retained the title Mother Agnes), Céline (now Sister Geneviéve), Marie of the Sacred Heart, and Thérèse's novice Marie of the Trinity were four who wrote down a great deal about Thérèse during these final months of her life, and their efforts are compiled in the marvelous book known in English as *Her Last Conversations*.

Thérèse died on September 30, 1897. One year later, the Carmel published 2,000 copies of her accidental autobiography, the memories she'd written under obedience and the few pages she had written on one particular occasion to her sister Marie. There were many skeptics among the nuns and the monastery's benefactors who wondered what in the world they would do with all those copies...

Leaving only enough time for the post to deliver the freshly printed pages, Sister Thérèse of the Child Jesus and the Holy Face, of the Carmel of Lisieux, France, became an immediate international sensation. As she had predicted from her sickbed, her sisters in the monastery would have no time to miss her; they would "find her in the mailbox." Sure enough, letters began to arrive from all over the world testifying to the intercession, the presence, and the friendship of Thérèse.

Her many new friends pressed for her Cause to be opened, and soon it was. She was beatified in 1923, canonized in 1925, proclaimed Principal Patroness of the Missions, on a par with St. Francis Xavier, in 1927, named Secondary Patroness of France, equal to St. Joan of Arc, in 1944, and proclaimed the 33rd Doctor of the Church in 1997.

And through all these years, she has not begun to rest but continues to "come down," fulfilling her mission to make God loved as she loves Him, even until the end of the world.

Appendix III

Recommended Reading

My fondness for good books was my salvation.

—Teresa of Avila, *The Book of Her Life*

I love to recommend books, and below you will find my recommended reading on St. Thérèse.

Remember that for complicated souls, there are no simple ways. Forget alphabetical order, then. I'm presenting my favorite books on St. Thérèse in the order in which I recommend them, though honestly, they're all so good, the order isn't that important. In a last ditch effort at simplicity, I'll say merely that I recommend *Story of a Soul* first, and *I Believe in Love* second. But finally, the best advice I can give is "Take what you like and leave the rest."

Let the Holy Spirit be your guide, and ask your guardian angel's assistance. God and your angel know your particular soul quite intimately, and they will guide you to just what you need, when you need it.

Finally, if there's a book or two on St. Thérèse that you love and don't see on my list, it's likely I haven't discovered it yet. There are so many wonderful books on her that I'm always finding new ones myself. And so, without further ado, here are my favorites.

Suzie's Suggested Life-Changing Books on St. Thérèse

Story of a Soul, St. Thérèse of Lisieux
 I recommend the edition translated by Fr. John Clarke, O.C.D. and published by ICS, the Institute of Carmelite Studies; they publish the best editions of Thérèse's original works, as well as other Carmelite classics.

I Believe in Love, Father Jean C.J. D'Elbée (Sophia Institute Press)
 This book is best described as a perennial favorite. My husband and I have given away many copies over the years, and again and again we've heard how Fr. D'Elbée's retreat conferences on Thérèse and her Little Way have transformed lives. If you want to walk the Little Way in freedom and joy, *I Believe in Love* will help you stay on the path.

The Autobiography of Brother Marcel Van (Amis de Van Éditions)
Conversations (with Jesus, Mary, and Thérèse), Marcel Van (Amis de Van Éditions)
 These two books are by the spiritual little brother of St. Thérèse, Servant of God Marcel Van. While both books are eminently worth reading, I recommend starting the *Autobiography* about two-thirds of the way through at (562) when, in October of 1942, this dear Vietnamese boy asked Thérèse to be his big sister. She responded by becoming not only his sister, but his personal tutor in her Little Way. In *Conversations*, Marcel obeys Jesus (and his spiritual director) and transcribes the many conversations he had with Jesus, Mary, and St. Thérèse. If you think this sounds too good to be true, you're almost correct. Jesus

named Marcel "the second Thérèse" and *Conversations,* alongside *Story of a Soul* and *I Believe in Love,* completes the perfect Little Way trilogy.

Soeur Thérèse of Lisieux, The Little Flower of Jesus
St. Thérèse of Lisieux, The Little Flower of Jesus
These two books were published before and after Thérèse's canonization respectively, and consist of her Autobiography, Counsels and Reminiscences, a selection of her Letters, Prayers, and Poems, "Shower of Roses," and the Process of Beatification and Canonization—the "shower of roses" varying between the two primary editions, and some supplementary material on the Processes varying as Souer Thérèse became Venerable, Blessed, and Saint. The editor was Fr. Thomas Taylor, a young Scottish priest who, having read an early edition of *Story of a Soul,* visited Mother Marie de Gonzague and Thérèse's sisters at the Lisieux Carmel in 1903 and was the first to suggest Thérèse's possible canonization. Fr. Taylor began publishing these books in 1912, and thousands upon thousands sold. I call them the "big Green books" and though they have long been out of print, they turn up with surprising frequency because of the huge number printed and sold. They are worth finding!

Thérèse of Lisieux and Marie of the Trinity, Pierre Descouvement (Alba House)
The Letters of St. Thérèse of Lisieux and Those Who Knew Her, tr. John Clarke, O.C.D. (Volumes I and II; ICS)
I recommend starting with Volume II.

St. Thérèse of Lisieux: Her Last Conversations, tr. John Clarke, O.C.D. (ICS)
Céline, Stéphane-Joseph Piat, O.F.M. (Ignatius Press)

A Memoir of My Sister, St. Thérèse, Sr. Geneviéve of the Holy
Face/Céline Martin (TAN Books)

Under the Torrent of His Love, Blessed Marie-Eugene of the Child
Jesus (Alba House)

Little Catechism of the Act of Oblation to Merciful Love, Carmel
of Lisieux/Céline and Pauline (Sophia Institute Press)

Complete Spiritual Doctrine of St. Thérèse of Lisieux, Francois
Jamart, O.C.D. (Alba House)

33 Days to Divine Mercy, Fr. Michael E. Gaitley, MIC (Marian Press)
Not only is this a wonderful book, but it has within its
pages the clearest eight photographs of St. Thérèse that
I've ever seen. And better yet (worth the price of the
book): the inside front cover is a gorgeous color repro-
duction of Céline's painting of the Holy Face from the
Shroud of Turin.

A Retreat with St. Thérèse, Pére Liagre, C.S.Sp

The Poetry of St. Thérèse of Lisieux, tr. Donald Kinney, O.C.D.
(ICS)

Maurice and Thérèse, The Story of a Love, Bishop Patrick Ahern
(Doubleday)

John and Thérèse: Flames of Love, Bishop Guy Gaucher, O.C.D.
(Alba House)

The Way of Trust and Love, Jacques Philippe (Scepter)

The Little Way of Saint Thérèse of Lisieux, John Nelson (Ligouri)

Thérèse of Lisieux, A Vocation of Love, Marie-Pascale Ducrocq
(Alba House)

Thoughts of St. Thérèse (originally from the Lisieux Carmel, 1915;
TAN Books)

The Prayers of St. Thérèse of Lisieux, tr. Aletheia Kane, O.C.D. (ICS)

The Plays of St. Thérèse of Lisieux, tr. Susan Conroy and David
J. Dwyer (ICS)

The Spirit of St. Thérèse de l'Enfant Jésus, (by Céline; out of print;
Burns, Oates, and Washbourne, London, 1925)

Beyond East and West, John C. H. Wu (Sheed and Ward, 1951; University of Notre Dame Press, 2018)

The Interior Carmel, John C. H. Wu (out of print; Sheed and Ward, 1953)

China: Lost Mission? Nicholas Maestrini, P. I.M.E. (Pime World Press)

Forever Love, God's Plan for Happiness, Nicholas Maestrini, P. I.M.E. (Pime World Press)
While this book and the three previous titles are not principally focused on St. Thérèse, they offer beautiful insights into her teaching and, especially, her intercession. John C. H. Wu was a convert who became the first Chinese ambassador to the Holy See, in 1947; St. Thérèse had played a big part in his conversion. Fr. Nicholas Maestrini, John Wu's spiritual father, shared with him an intense love for St. Thérèse, whom Father Maestrini had "met" when he served as an altar boy in Rome at her beatification and canonization. He, like Pope Pius XI, called little Thérèse "the guiding star" of his life. It was, incidentally, Céline who introduced me to John Wu, who in turn (through his book *Beyond East and West*) introduced me to Fr. Maestrini. Hence my conviction that good books make good friends.

The Intimate Life of Saint Thérèse, Portrayed by Those Who Knew Her, Albert H. Dolan, O.Carm (Loreto Publications)
Fr. Dolan founded the National Shrine of the Little Flower in Chicago, Illinois and the Society of the Little Flower now based in Darien, Illionois. He traveled frequently to France to spend time with (and obtain relics from) Thérèse's sisters Mother Agnes (Pauline), Marie, Céline, and Leonie. This book is a compilation of mission sermons he preached at the National Shrine in the 1930s, and contains the conversations Fr. Dolan had with the Martin sisters, as well as their messages to those wanting to follow the Little Way.

St. Thérèse, Doctor of the Little Way (Franciscan Friars of the
Immaculate)
The Power of Confidence, Conrad De Meester, O.C.D. (Alba
House)
Léonie Martin, Marie Baudouin-Croix (Veritas)
The Story of a Life, Bishop Guy Gaucher, O.C.D. (Harper Collins)
Holy Daring: The Fearless Trust of St. Thérèse of Lisieux, John
Udris (Pauline Books)
I Thirst, Saint Thérèse of Lisieux and Mother Teresa of Calcutta,
Jacques Gauthier (Alba House)
The Photo Album of Saint Thérèse of Lisieux (Christian Classics)
Thérèse and Lisieux, Pierre Descouvement & Helmuth Nils Loose
(Novalis)
Saint Thérèse of Lisieux: Her Life, Times, and Teaching, Conrad
De Meester, O.C.D, ed. (ICS)
*St. Thérèse of Lisieux by those who knew her, Testimonies from the
process of beatification*, ed. and tr. by Christopher O. Mahony,
O.C.D. (Our Sunday Visitor)
I recommend this book with reservations. For myself, I
have found it to be daunting. Reading about Thérèse's
heroic virtue with no break for her humor and littleness
can be hazardous to the Little Way. I suggest, then, that
if you can't resist reading it, you try not to plow straight
through. Ask Thérèse's intercession before you start; and
intersperse your reading with pages from some of the titles
above— *I Believe in Love*, for instance, or *Story of a Soul*.

Thérèse, the Little Child of God's Mercy, Àngel de les Gavarres
(ICS)
This book comes last not because it's the last book I
recommend, but because it's the last book Thérèse recommended to me. I discovered it just after I finished
writing this manuscript, and it confirmed everything I
had discovered. Thank you, little Thérèse!

Bibliography

Àngel de les Gavarres. *Thérèse, the Little Child of God's Mercy.* Washington, D.C.: ICS Publications, 1999.

Anthony Mary Claret. *The Autobiography of St. Anthony Mary Claret.* Rockford, Illinois: TAN Books and Publishers, Inc., 1985.

Belanger, Dina. *Canticle of Love: Autobiography of Marie Sainte-Cecile de Rome, R.J.M.* Sillery, Quebec: Convent of Jesus and Mary, 1961.

Bertone, Cardinal Tarcisio. *The Last Secret of Fatima.* New York: Doubleday, 2008

Carrico, James A. *The Life of Venerable Mary of Agreda.* Stockbridge, MA: Marian Press, 1959.

Congregation Pro Clericis. *Eucharistic Adoration for the Sanctification of Priests and Spiritual Maternity.* Fort Collins, CO: Roman Catholic Books, 2013.

D'Elbée, Fr. Jean C.J. *I Believe in Love.* Manchester, New Hampshire: Sophia Institute Press, 2001.

Descouvemont, Pierre. *Thérèse of Lisieux and Marie of the Trinity*. New York: Alba House, 1997.

Echevarria, Juan. *The Miracles of St. Anthony Mary Claret*. Rockford, Illinois: TAN Books and Publishers, Inc., 1992

Flynn, Vinnie. *7 Secrets of the Eucharist*. Stockbridge, MA: Marian Press.

Fr. Tarcisio of Cervinara. *Padre Pio's Mass*. San Giovanni Rotondo, Italy: "The Voice of Padre Pio" Editions, 2003.

Gaitley, Michael E. *33 Days to Merciful Love*. Stockbridge, MA: Marian Press, 2016.

———. *33 Days to Morning Glory*. Stockbridge, MA: Marian Press, 2013.

Gaucher, Guy. *John and Thérèse: Flames of Love*. New York: Alba House, 1999.

Holy Bible. (Translations used in this book include RSV and New American.)

Jamart, Rev. Francois. *Complete Spiritual Doctrine of St. Thérèse of Lisieux*. New York: Alba House, 1961.

Kowalska, Saint Maria Faustina. *Diary: Divine Mercy in My Soul*. Stockbridge, MA: Marian Press, 2011.

Lozano, John M. *Anthony Claret: A Life in the Service of the Gospel*. Chicago: Claretian Publications, 1985.

———. *Mystic and Man of Action: Saint Anthony Mary Claret*. Chicago: Claretian Publications, 1977.

Marie-Eugene of the Child Jesus. *Under the Torrent of His Love*. New York: Alba House, 1995.

Mary of Agreda. *City of God: The Coronation*. Washington, NJ: Ave Maria Institute, 1971.

Oder, Slawomir, and Salverio Gaeta. *Why He is a Saint*. New York: Rizzoli, 2010.

O'Mahony, Christopher. *St. Thérèse of Lisieux by those who knew her*. Huntington, IN: Our Sunday Visitor, Inc., 1975.

Petitot, O.P., Henry. *Saint Teresa of Lisieux, A Spiritual Renascence.* London: Burns Oates & Washbourne, Ltd., 1927.

Sister Geneviève of the Holy Face (Céline Martin). *Memoir of My Sister, St. Thérèse.* New York: P.J. Kenedy & Sons, 1959.

The Spirit of Saint Thérèse de l'Enfant Jésus: As shown forth by her Writings and the Testimony of Eyewitnesses. London: Burns Oates & Washbourne, Ltd., 1925.

Taylor, T.N. *Soeur Thérèse of Lisieux.* New York: P.J. Kenedy & Sons, 1922.

Teresa of Avila. *Collected Works, Volume One: The Book of Her Life; Spiritual Testimonies; Soliloquies.* Washington, D.C.: ICS Publications, 1987.

Thérèse of Lisieux. *General Correspondence, Vol. II.* Washington, D.C.: ICS Publications, 1988.

———. *Last Conversations.* Washington, D.C.: ICS Publications, 1977.

———. *The Prayers of Saint Thérèse of Lisieux.* Washington, D.C.: ICS Publications, 1997.

———. *Story of a Soul.* Washington, D.C.: ICS Publications, 1996.

Van, Marcel. *Autobiography.* Versailles: Amis De Van Éditions, 2017.

Van Speybrouck, Edward. *Father Paul of Moll.* Rockford, IL: TAN Books and Publishers, Inc., 1979.

Vie Thérésienne (Thérésian Life), N. 74 (April 1979); N. 77 (January 1980).

Acknowledgments

When I pray for you, I don't say a 'Pater' or an 'Ave' for you,
I say simply, lifting up my heart to God:
"O my God, grant my little brothers and sisters
all kinds of good things;
and if You can, love them even more."

—St. Thérèse and Suzie

First, thanks to the holy priests who have assisted me with this book: Fr. Donald Kinney, O.C.D., for his interest and support from the beginning, his kindness and expertise in reading the manuscript, his suggestions for improving it, and his conviction that this book is important; and Monsignor Kenneth Loughman, for his outrageous enthusiasm for my outrageous idea, his timely interventions to promulgate the manuscript, and his insistence that I publish this book.

Second, I am grateful for the professional advice and warm-hearted response to *Something New* that I received from Aja McCarthy, Margot Davidson, Mike Aquilina, and Christine

Jensen. My thanks also to D.Q. McInerny and Sister Natalie for their kind permission to use their words on the back cover.

Third, profound thanks to the amazing team at Little Way Books: especially Miriam Schroder and Nora Malone. Also my gratitude to Nathalie Mengeot in Lisieux who, with the help of Sylvie and Victoire, obtained for me the copies of *Vie Thérésienne* I needed, and the copyright permission for our cover image. May God and St. Thérèse reward you all with roses beyond measure!

My deep gratitude also to Maura McKeegan, Cynthia Montanaro, and Rose Wong and the Secular Discalced Carmelites of St Thérèse in Westlake Village, for prayers and encouragement. Words can't convey my heartfelt thanks to Mary Anne Birch for letting me read aloud and talk over the contents of this book, and to Karen Collins for her warm reception of the same.

I am eternally grateful to Jack Keogan for his translations of Marcel Van, and to Charlene Richard for showing up at the eleventh hour.

Last but far from least, thanks to my husband Tony, whose assurances that Thérèse's idea was new and important, and that this book had to be written, have made it happen.

About the Author

*Jesus is full of tenderness; it pleases Him a lot to
welcome our marks of love, whatever they are.*

—Marcel Van

Suzie Andres is a Catholic wife and mother who lives and writes
in Southern California, where her husband Tony teaches at their
alma mater, Thomas Aquinas College.

Her previous books are *The Paradise Project*, a romantic com-
edy for all ages; two books about homeschooling; and a book of
sermons by Fr. Thomas Aquinas McGovern, S.J. She currently
writes about "the second St. Thérèse," Servant of God Marcel
Van, at suzieandres.com/blog.

Something New with St. Thérèse launches a new publishing
label, Little Way Books, on the 125th anniversary of St. Thérèse's
Act of Oblation to Merciful Love.

179